# forging mettle

## Praise for *Forging Mettle*

'It is said that the only limit for a company's growth is the ambition of its founder. The story of Nrupender Rao's life and work in *Forging Mettle* describes his journey over seven decades. I have known him for many years and have witnessed Pennar's evolution, from a steel converter to an engineering firm, as Nrupender guided it through its ups and downs by his foundational principle of putting people first. I recommend this book to all who believe that entrepreneurship and optimism are the mechanism by which we can create enduring institutions.'

**Sajjan Jindal, chairman, JSW Group**

'For many entrepreneurs, the definition of a successful business is high profitability, liquidity and market capitalization. Nrupender Rao and Pennar's story presents a unique philosophy for a company which is rooted in doing good and being good. I recommend this book to all aspiring entrepreneurs who want to understand how to build a principled and ethical institution.'

**Arunachalam Vellayan, vice chairman, Murugappa Group**

'The entrepreneurial journey of Nrupender Rao in *Forging Mettle* gives the reader a front-row seat in the roller coaster ride of starting a company, getting great traction, facing sudden seemly insurmountable challenges and existential risks and to finally overcoming them. This book exemplifies his never say die spirit and his total commitment to ethical management and job creation. In a country like India, one sometimes wonders if it's possible to build an institution that is profitable, principled and kind. Nrupender Rao's lifetime of work has been his attempt to answer that question.'

**B.V.R. Mohan Reddy, founder chairman and board member, Cyient**

'Driven by innovation and technologies ahead of their times to serve unmet needs of the industry and society, here is a dynamic entrepreneur from my city, Hyderabad, who built multiple businesses in the last several decades. Nrupender Rao's journey has not been linear and has had its highs and lows, but what is consistent throughout is his commitment to principles and ethical ways of doing business. He has shown that ethical entrepreneurship can create tremendous value to all stakeholders.'

**G.V. Prasad, co-chairman and managing director,**
**Dr Reddy's Laboratories**

# forging mettle

## Nrupender Rao and the Pennar Story

PAVAN C. LALL

HARPER
BUSINESS
*An Imprint of* HarperCollins *Publishers*

First published in India by Harper Business
An imprint of HarperCollins *Publishers* 2022
4th Floor, Tower A, Building No. 10, Phase II, DLF Cyber City,
Gurugram, Haryana – 122002
www.harpercollins.co.in

2 4 6 8 10 9 7 5 3 1



P-ISBN: 978-93-9440-722-0
E-ISBN: 978-93-9440-723-7



Typeset in 13/18 Minion Pro at
Manipal Technologies Limited, Manipal

Printed and bound at
Thomson Press (India) Ltd

FSC MIX Paper FSC® C010615

This book is produced from independently certified FSC® paper to ensure responsible forest management.

*To my father,*
*P.C. Lall (1943–2007)*

# Contents

*Courage is the first of human qualities because it is the quality which guarantees the others.*

*—Aristotle*

# Author's Note

I first came to Hyderabad sometime in 2011 and was fascinated by the city's rich culture and heritage. The region is showcased to the outside world through its cuisine, through its splendid legacy of royalty, and as the origin of some of the world's finest diamonds. These were what drew me to Hyderabad more than a decade ago. The last few times I visited the city, however, were not for the food or the history. I was in Hyderabad to tell the story of Nrupender Rao and the company he founded—Pennar.

I began the project late last year and was initially under the impression that this would turn out to be yet another story about a not-so-rich man making a fortune, or the story of triumph emerging from disaster. Sure, any business story in India is a story of triumph in a country where the ease of business was a challenge in and of itself—even though things have gotten better. But the story I discovered in Hyderabad was something quite different.

I found myself telling the tale of the victory of the human spirit against the most difficult of odds and the will to do it whilst not compromising on values and principles. That is hard enough to do while one is hale and hearty. Nrupender Rao has done all this while coping with a debilitating health condition.

As a writer who has authored books on corporate blow-ups, I was keen on telling a different kind of story, an inspirational story if you will. And unlike the more common narratives around winning and how to succeed, I wanted to write about something that was inspirational and provided business leaders and aspirants alike lessons that are less discussed and spoken about.

The promoters of the book gave me a free hand in shaping this story and telling it in the most authentic way possible, while offering research support and background information relevant to the journey. The result was a project that not only allowed me to depict the Pennar story but also served to answer the many questions I have had as an author of business books in the past, and I hope will do the same for others who are in the business world.

I owe particular thanks to Aditya Rao and the entire Rao family for their cooperation, patience and understanding in allowing me to work in the way I wanted to. They not only opened their homes to me, but freely gave me information and insights all through the journey. Pennar's ex-employees and friends are all owed a note of thanks for their role in taking this book to completion, as are my editors Sachin Sharma and Shreya Lall and the entire team at HarperCollins. Thank you, Sunil Kuram, for your constant presence and advice, and the most memorable roadside dosa lunch we had en route to the factories.

Brinda Vasudevan, who is a friend and former editor of mine, deserves special mention for her keen insight and special talent for guiding me on the finer nuances of storytelling, as is Deepa Krishnamurthy, who offered sage support in helping me better comprehend the way businesses in South India work as well as differ from the rest of India. The entire team at ITC Hotels in Hyderabad where I visited and stayed while I worked and travelled to write this book needs express mention for their support and guidance in navigating the city.

For my family that includes my mother, my brothers—Vikash and Siddarth—and RJD for their unflinching support and encouragement for all my projects.

This book is the outcome of a reporter's sensitivity and the insights from a business house's experience and knowledge. Whether the nobleness of bringing both those views to fruition has been achieved may best be judged by you, the reader.

# An Offer That Could Not Be Refused

In the summer of 1989, Vijay Puljal, a minor shareholder and a business advisor who was part of Nrupender Rao's inner circle, received a call from the Hyderabad branch of Grindlays from a Mr Mukherjee. Mukherjee, the manager of the bank, asked if the company was interested in selling shares of Nagarjuna Signode where Nrupender Rao was the chief promoter and owned around 10 per cent of the firm. The company had other investors which included Nagarjuna Steel, Chicago-based Signode Corp and IFC-Washington. Puljal, an agricultural scientist by training specializing in entomology, passed on the message to Rao, who was offshore in Dubai for a business meeting. 'We are not interested' was the flat reply and the message was conveyed to Mukherjee. Precisely sixty minutes later, Puljal got a call at his investment office in Chikoti Gardens, Begumpet. He picked up the receiver of the table phone and was partially surprised to hear Mukherjee on the line again. 'The price of your shares is being quoted at Rs 150 in the market. We can offer you a premium above the market price at Rs 200 per share for 1,00,000 shares,' he said to Puljal. That sort of a bid would give Rao and his team a premium of Rs 50 lakh on a Rs 2 crore sale of shares.

Puljal politely declined, keeping Rao's direction on the matter in mind, and put the phone down. He also tried to reach Rao once again, but the receptionist at his hotel said he was occupied in a meeting and would get free later in the evening.

After thirty minutes, Puljal got into his maroon-coloured 118 NE Fiat, went home—in Somajiguda, a ten-minute drive away—and had his customary light lunch consisting of vegetables, rice and dal, and then returned to the office. Hardly had he sat down at his desk when the phone rang once more and it was Mukherjee again. This time, Puljal recalled that the caller had jacked up his offer to Rs 300 per share, effectively doubling the market value of the deal. That took Puljal by surprise, and his mind snapped into action as he realized that this was more than just an equity-diversification play by the bank. There was more happening under the surface. He paused. Then asked the voice on the other side of the phone flatly, 'Whose interests are you really representing?' There was a long silence before Mukherjee answered: 'It is a stockbroker from Calcutta. That is all I can say.' Puljal exhaled and said he would check and get back. Again he called Dubai and passed on a message to Rao who was in a board meeting, while Puljal was kept on hold. The operator came back in a minute and told him that 'Mr Rao's position on the matter was the same.'

Puljal called Mukherjee back and repeated what he had said a couple of hours earlier. 'I am very sorry, but our management is not interested. I wish you good luck.' He ordered his afternoon cup of tea and turned his attention to pending matters. Thirty minutes before the markets closed, the phone rang yet again. Puljal answered.

It was Mukherjee again, insisting that they consider the transaction. Puljal, by now in a hurry to leave the office and running out of patience with Mukherjee, threw out an absurd figure to mostly get him off his back. 'We can consider your offer if you can pay Rs 500 *and* the condition is that the brokerage fees of Rs 50,000 or 1 per cent would be paid to Grindlays Bank and that the bank would give them an official statement on their letterhead verifying all details of the deal.' Mukherjee said he would get back. Puljal thought that if he said yes, which was a one in a million chance, he would figure out how to convince Rao to agree to the deal.

Puljal, by then, had wound down for the day and was putting his papers into his briefcase so he could head out when, to his surprise, the phone rang.

'We are okay with that price, and I am coming to your office with the letter stating your terms and conditions. Will you please wait there?' Mukherjee asked. Forty-five minutes later, the man from Grindlays showed up. He was heavyset, fair and on the short side and carried the letter, as discussed, with the additional condition that payment would be made within thirty days.

The next day, Rao returned to Hyderabad, and in their briefings at his office, Puljal explained what had happened and how they were sitting on a windfall gain of 200 per cent on the market price. Rao thought for a second before saying, 'Well, if you have taken that call and made a commitment, then we are obliged to honour it.'

Thirty days later, Puljal went to Calcutta with two suitcases full of share certificates and returned with a demand draft for Rs 4,99,50,000.

# 1

# Buffalo Taxis, River Showers and Lantern Weddings

## October 2021, Hyderabad

No amount of experience in the trenches of dyed-in-the-wool journalism could have taught me what to expect when I was told I would be driven down to meet the patriarch of Pennar Industries, Nrupender Rao, at his home. Preliminary research had already shown me that he was highly educated and sophisticated, and had worked in international markets. He was a first-generation entrepreneur who had launched and ran businesses in diverse industries both before and after liberalization of the Indian economy in the nineties. It was no small concern that he was also fighting a serious neurological condition that was impacting his ability to walk and speak. He had already shared his observations about life in a bullet point format with me in a bid to help me tell his story and describe his trials and tribulations.

Yet, myriad questions swam in my mind as I tried to assess how I would be able to get answers from him. My car ride to his residence in Jubilee Hills, an upscale residential part of Hyderabad, did not take more than thirty minutes. Then we reached his home—a large double-storied structure—and after repeated introductions, three times to be precise, we were finally let into the premises.

I walked into a huge living room on the first floor. It is large enough to seat thirty people with safety norms that would make the WHO proud. The owner of the home was seated in what was either a recliner or a wheelchair. I could not tell for sure.

He had a light cashmere shawl wrapped around him and was clearly fighting his illness. His hands gnarled and by his sides, but the expression on his face could not be mistaken for anything else but hospitality and welcome, and then the look in his eyes left no room for doubt. Rao looked straight at me, in the same friendly manner as childhood friends who have known you since kindergarten might do. He was clearly alert and entirely aware of who I was, possessed with almost as much curiosity as me.

As far as I could tell, he had a thousand questions circling in his mind, his judgement processing how this might play out in the long run. Would it be an enjoyable voyage that might lead him to stumble on interesting insights and lessons and turn the exercise into one of renewed self-discovery, or would it be an underwhelming one in futility, which was the last thing he ought to be wasting his precious time on. That is exactly the point at which I could not stop the yard-wide smile on my face because it was abundantly clear that he was simply projecting a reflection of everything that he was seeing on my face. His daughters, son and other family members sat around us as introductions were made, but his eyes stayed focused, hardly ever shifting from me. The next two hours allowed me to ask questions and get a deeper understanding of the life of the person sitting in front of me, but, in many ways, it was also a silent and complex interview that I was undertaking.

---

November 1957. The soft, dewy stillness of the village dawn is shattered by the sound of a rooster crowing, nature's alarm clock signalling that the dark night is over and that a new day has dawned. Minutes later, a street dog, lower in the social order of morning sentinels, barks. Once, then twice. Then a succession of howls seems to last forever. The creaking of a bicycle—probably a farmer on his way to deliver milk to those families that did not own cattle.

It is early winter, and the family is fast asleep in the rambling haveli in the Adilabad district of Andhra Pradesh (now Telangana). Only a twelve-year-old boy is awake. He knows there will be activity in the kitchen, so he rubs the sleep from his eyes and tiptoes downstairs, leaving his brother and four sisters still sleeping. He wanders through the spacious rooms designed for large, joint families and ends up in the kitchen where the family cook is already preparing for lunch.

He watches sleepily as the cook brings in a plastic bucket of water in which silvery Pulasa fish are swimming. Godavari Pulasa, known elsewhere as hilsa, is a freshwater fish that is available in the monsoon season. It is a delicacy in all the villages close to the Godavari River. The boy has so far seen Pulasa only on his plate. Now, however, he watches in horrified fascination as the cook pulls out one of the silvery fish and washes it. The fish writhes in agony and struggles to break free of the iron grasp. But the cook has clearly been doing this for years, and he does not loosen his grip till the fish stops its struggle, its eyes wide open, frozen in mute suffering.

When the lunch is served, the boy eats rice, vegetables and curd. The incident ensures that he never eats fish again.

That day, the young Nrupender Rao understood the reality of the great food chain of life. Visiting his grandparents at their ancestral home meant vast feasts of meat, poultry and, of course, fish. Fish, in particular, was readily available since the village was close to the river. But having seen what it costs to get it onto his plate, the young boy had lost his appetite for fish.

Back in those days, electricity, water and transport—the utilities that most citizens take for granted today—were bona fide luxuries for most of India. Even as the larger cities got familiar with the railway network, aircraft and motor cars, small towns dealt with power outages or power vacuums, regions with no road connectivity or motorable infrastructure and the still dreamed of network of piped water. In many ways, life in the villages has not changed much.

None of this had an impact on the young Rao. What he did know was that to get to his grandfather's home in Dwaraka village in Adilabad (not the infinitely more famous place in Gujarat), his family had to take a train from Hyderabad to Mancherial, where a bullock cart would be waiting to convey them some forty kilometres to the village. There were no taxis or autorickshaws back then. Only wood wheels, a flatbed and farm animals to ferry them to their destination.

Rao's paternal grandfather, Gopal Rao, was known in the village as a hardworking, farming-focused and mirthful landowner. When it came to his family, Gopal Rao preferred that his son be an agriculturalist and a landlord as opposed to pursuing advanced education. His eldest son, J.V. Narsing Rao, was adamantly inclined towards higher learning and went on to graduate from Aligarh University. He subsequently attended Banaras Hindu University for his master's and law degrees. Narsing Rao then practised law in Hyderabad, returning to his village occasionally.

From when he was seven till when he was around fifteen years old, Rao and his family made that trip back in time to the village—bumping along cobbled streets for the better part of three hours to get to the sprawling ancestral home. They would also make a trip to their maternal grandparents in Narsingapuram.

While, for the young Nrupender, the sight of the fish being killed was something he would remember all his life, he was too young to be aware then of the far more impactful and historical events that had taken place a scant ten years before.

---

Let us travel back in time to the 1930s. The British ruled India, but they allowed hundreds of princely states to exist. These princely states and their rulers were fractious, with splits, breakaways and meltdowns happening in large and small empires across the land. The prime example was Hyderabad under its Nizam. Once considered amongst the foremost princely states, Hyderabad had come to be known as a textbook example of autocratic rule and feudalistic government.

But the world did not see it the same way. On Monday, 22 February 1937, *Time* magazine put His Exalted Highness Sir Mir Osman Ali Khan, the Nizam of Hyderabad and Berar, on the cover with a story inside that opened with the following description: 'India has no native state so rich, potent and extensive as Hyderabad which is about the size of the United Kingdom and there, last week, the Royal Family of the Asatia Dynasty celebrated the Silver Jubilee of "The Richest Man in the World".'

The magazine went on to describe how 'the "State of Hyderabad", the "Heart of the Indian Peninsula", occupies the centre of the continental globe. Unusually fertile and desert-free, it is dotted with artificial lakes and storage reservoirs, has no sea coast—a grave disadvantage—but is well-watered by a system of rivers on which float many a quaint coracle. The district drains eastward into the Bay of Bengal.' All of this was to tell the reader about how the state was naturally abundant with resources and was self-sustaining both economically and agriculturally.

Hyderabad was one of the hundreds of princely states that functioned alongside British-governed India. Each of these states made treaties with the representative of the Crown in India on everything from border issues to the functioning of the railways and the postal department. The British created the Chamber of Princes, a group that would represent the interest of the various princely states, debate issues and settle on policies and objectives that would advance the common interests of British India as well as of Princely India. The chamber had both an advisory and a consultative position. The 565 royal families were represented by 120 princes led by a chancellor who had to be a member prince.

Larger and more powerful princely states, such as Hyderabad, Mysore and Baroda, stayed aloof from the Chamber of Princes. They assumed that their size and self-sufficiency meant that they did not need the power of the collective. Even as the chamber faced its own problems, with its long-time chairman—the Maharaja of Patiala—deciding to resign, the British conducted the first elections in India in 1937 as a step towards provincial autonomy.

The ruling princes, from the shadowy privacy of their courts and councils, watched these elections with great interest. The Indian National Congress won those elections, but World War II began a couple of years later, and India was pulled into the war because of the British.

The Nizam of Hyderabad was not unaware of all that was going on around him. He had decided to join the new India when it was created and become a part of the rest of the country. However, by 1947, the Nizam had a change of heart and decided that he wanted Hyderabad to function as an independent state and not accede to the newly created India. But, by then, his sway over the state had diminished for multiple reasons that notably included the rise of the Telangana movement.

Consequently, in 1948, the Indian army sent in its troops and invaded Hyderabad. The state was annexed, and the Nizam was given no choice but to surrender, after which he was given a titular role. As the Rajpramukh of Hyderabad (an administrative title like governor), he continued to assume a somewhat receding figurehead-like role between 1950 and 1956. Then the state was partitioned and carved into Andhra Pradesh, Karnataka and Maharashtra.

---

At a very young age, during the Razaakar movement and other subsequent upheavals, Nrupender's father would send him, his sisters and his mother to Pithapuram in Andhra for their safety, all the while refusing to go with them despite the risks. They were sent there because the socio-political movements had not reached that part of the state, and their families and relatives would be relatively insulated.

But the boy, Nrupender, was too young to understand how these larger political issues would impact his life. Back in the 1950s, the things that mattered to him were more localized.

He recalls the sense of community in the village. 'On several of my visits to the village, we would have all-night music sessions where there would be devotional songs sung within the local communities at get-togethers that went on and on for several hours,' Rao says. These get-togethers—collectively referred to as Margali—were indicative of an auspicious month that started sometime in December-January and centred mostly around spiritual activities. That and Bathukamma, a festival where the women sang and danced to devotional music, were central to communal activities in the village.

Beyond religion and music, there were other recreational opportunities for young ones that were perhaps absent in the bigger, still developing metropolises across the nation.

The Godavari River was all of one mile away from the village and was a godsend for both adults and little children in a world that was still devoid of technology, and would be for many years. Rao and his siblings would hop across to the river mainly for a bath and sometimes to simply splash around and have some fun.

'We had no indoor plumbing at home, so we would go to the river to bathe. In those days, the village was not electrified, and the roads were not paved,' Rao recalls. There was no shortage of family members and locals who were innovative enough to make life work for them irrespective of the challenges in infrastructure.

'I lived in a two-storied house in the village, and I remember the woodcarvings and the specific areas where rice and grain was stored—a common feature of homes in the village then,' he says, alluding to the fact that the network of grocery stores and local food suppliers was either not yet developed or sparse in the hinterland.

The norms of everyday life then, compared to now, would almost seem like an exercise in pantomime. Take something as simple as attending a wedding at night. The barely paved roads were unlit; there were no street lights as there are today. What that meant was when a family was attending a ceremony, they would have an attendant who would run in front of the cart with a lantern in his hand to show the way.

Back in the city after those simpler times in the village, the young Rao began to understand the complexities of the world around him—caste, class, eating habits and mannerisms. 'My grandfather would send three cooks from the village to the city, four months a turn, to cook for us,' Rao recalls. On one particular weekend, he remembers, a friend dropped in. 'We gave him a crispy fried snack to eat, and he enjoyed it thoroughly at that point in time.' The boy asked what the snack was made of. 'Minced meat' was the reply. The boy, his eyes dilated wide, his expression one of horror, rushed from the room and could be heard vomiting. It turned out that the friend was a Brahmin and a vegetarian, and his life was determined by lifestyle, ritualism and what he did or did not eat. For Rao, who belonged to a family that was religious but not puritanical, when it came to diet and lifestyle, what he ate meant nothing. But this incident stayed with him.

On another occasion, a repairman had come to the family house for an odd job. The young Rao ran up to him as he was hammering a nail into the wall and grabbed the man's hand to help him. His grandfather saw this and swept the little boy up and carried him into another room. There, Rao was admonished and told that what he had done was wrong and that he needed to take a bath immediately to cleanse himself. 'I did not understand how touching a man could be a taboo, but I understood that was not acceptable,' Rao recalls.

A vast majority of Hindus have the belief that a person is born into one of the four castes based on karma and past life. The traditional definition and categories of the castes go thus: Brahmins are priests or teachers, Kshatriyas are rulers and warriors, Vaishyas are merchants and men of commerce, and Shudras are the labour class.

Even within these four castes, there are scores of sub-castes that are further defined by geographic province and many other variables. Outside of those four broad categories has existed, and shamefully, a category considered so low that it does not justify segmentation within the existing framework. That is the category of outcastes or what the history books refer to as the 'Untouchables'.

Despite being based on religious principles practised over 1200 years ago, the system persists even today. For a boy who was being raised in a metropolitan city—even in the fifties—it was jarring to come up against such a practice, and something that he would remember to resist and break away from in the years ahead.

Rao's younger sister, Renuka, who was born two years after him and is the closest to him in age, is one of the few amongst his siblings who recalled visiting their family home in the country. 'I was his sidekick,' she says, adding that she would accompany him to various places and watch as he flew kites, helped hold the spinning wheel while he would navigate the manja, the finely coloured string that was coated with glass dust and used as a weapon to cut other kites down mid-flight.

Back home, she and her brother would trace out words that were etched into the walls by their lawyer father. 'Empathy, compassion, evolution and progressive' were some of the words that Rao scribbled in pencil in a bid to keep their meaning and resonance at the top of his mind. There were other terms that were more complex and part of the legal lexicon that meant nothing to the young children. But memories of those words would come back to them as they grew older and learnt more.

Rao was no stranger to books and reading, thanks to his parents who made learning a priority. He would regularly win academic prizes in school; many of those prizes were books, which the boy devoured. He would carry some of them to the village on occasion and read while the rest of the family slept—late in the evening and early in the morning. And like every avid reader has done as a child, he too had a small battery-operated torch which he used under the covers when the lights were officially switched off.

While life in the country had its own lessons, Rao and his siblings grew up for the most part in Hyderabad, changing their homes as their father's career progressed and he moved up the political hierarchy in the city and the state.

Chirag Ali Lane in Hyderabad is today a busy commercial centre flooded with mobile phone shops and retail outlets. Back in the 1950s, it was a residential enclave that was home to a diverse cross-section of residents that, amongst others, also included Ismaili Muslims, followers of the Aga Khan.

For young Rao, the neighbouring sports venue at Fateh Ali Maidan was a pleasant distraction where he and others would play cricket.

Suresh Kulkarni, former vice president for an engineering company that worked for NASA, now retired, recalls that his friendship with Nrupender—commonly referred to as 'Nrup' by his pals—began in 1951, when he transferred from All Saints' High School in Gunfoundry to Little Flower High School on Chirag Ali Lane. 'I recall that his home was just down the road, a few hundred yards from our school and sometimes during the lunch hour, I would go to his home to eat sweets and crisp South Indian snacks,' remembers Kulkarni.

He adds that he shared a particular sibling rivalry with Rao—they were constantly competing for the top position in class in junior high school and often traded first and second positions in their annual exams. The rivalry, however, started and ended in the classroom only on matters of academics.

Kulkarni was not the only one to feel at home at Rao's parents' house. Avula Bharath Bhushan, who met Rao a couple of years later in the third grade, says his friend was almost always leading the pack when it came to classes, which was at least one reason everyone was chasing him for clues on examinations. 'The other was that his home was so close to the school that we would jump out between sessions to go play table tennis there on the dining table, eat lunch and then head back for the next class,' Bhushan adds.

At that point, Rao's father was the president of the Indian National Congress for the state of Andhra Pradesh, but his home was no lavish gigantic mansion. 'There were perhaps just three rooms in the whole house,' says Rao's youngest sister, Rupa. She added that the family never saw their home as anything beyond a place to stay together. The fringe luxuries and amenities were never a pursuit of priority for the Raos.

The family stayed in the Chirag Ali Lane house only for a few years. They moved to Begumpet when their father was appointed minister for the Public Works Department under the cabinet and office of the then Chief Minister Neelam Sanjiva Reddy. Reddy would go on to become the seventh President of India in 1977 serving with Prime Ministers Morarji Desai, Charan Singh and Indira Gandhi, at different times.

Begumpet then was unlike the upscale, vibrant residential district that it is now. Back in the late fifties and sixties, it was a far-flung, isolated suburb of the city. But there were benefits that included a garden, orchards with mango and guava trees, security guards and a house with six bedrooms. That did not assuage Rao and his sisters, who were peeved that they had to travel an hour to get to school and to their favourite haunts on Abid Road. Abids, rumoured to be named after an Armenian merchant who was the Nizam's valet, was a major commercial circuit in the city, close to the post office, railway stations, restaurants, hotels and bustling markets.

The children were dropped off at school by their mother, who was then studying for a master's degree in Telugu. Once her classes were over, she would pick the kids up and ferry them home. The journeys back and forth in a light blue Ambassador car were tiring at first but kids being kids, they got used to it soon enough, finding the lighter side of life in their travels.

The Begumpet years came to an end soon, as J.V.N. Rao lost his ministry in the changing tides of Andhra's politics. The Raos had to move out of the fancy digs which came with the ministerial post. 'We moved houses so many times,' recalls Rupa. Clearly, their father thought so too and decided to build a house in the city. While that was being built, the family moved to a rented property that belonged to Annam Vishwanathan, a family friend.

The new house that was constructed in Domalguda was more in line with their Chirag Ali Lane dwelling. It was designed with modest features, with not very many rooms and starkly reflected how the head of the household just refused to be driven by material wealth. In fact, for Rao's father, the only mission worth pursuing—no matter what the cost—was education. India in the fifties was still developing its educational systems.

It was abundantly clear in the Rao household that while sports and other pursuits were encouraged, the primacy of academics and education was never in question. That common thread ran through the household regardless of gender, which was rare in Andhra and in the wider Indian context. Telugu society, like many others, has historically been both feudal and patriarchal in its structure.

Rao really had no choice but to do well in school. He went on to stay at the top of his class in the state board examinations and stood seventh in the entire state. Because he was academically gifted, Rao had been 'double-promoted'. As a result, he was too young for university when he finished high school. Instead of wasting a year, Rao opted for a pre-university course in science at Nizam College for a year before he was ready to apply to university. The boy was getting ready to face the world.

# 2

# Becoming a Minister's Son, Many Houses and a Foundation for the Future

**B**ACK IN THE CLASSROOM, A YOUNG NRUPENDER RAO IN Hyderabad got down to business, acing his grades, sitting in the front row and never missing a day of school. Sometimes, his teachers would end up missing class. When that happened, students were divided into groups and would quiz or debate each other.

Once, when a teacher was absent, the principal sent Tulja Ram Singh, known as Pandit-ji, to oversee the class. Pandit-ji was a tilak-wearing faculty member who decided to test the students with something unexpected. The students were eagerly waiting for him to suggest a quiz or a debate, and he obliged—with a twist. He suggested that they debate—in any language of their choice.

The students squirmed in their wooden seats. Should they pick Hindi, which was being spoken as the national language, or should they stick to Telugu, which was the mother tongue for most? What if they chose to debate in a language nobody understood? Worse, what if the other side debated in a language they did not understand? Also, Pandit-ji was not a native Telugu speaker. Should they debate in a language he would understand?

As his classmates were floundering for a solution to the language issue (which, to be fair, still comes up from time to time, even at the national level, because not everyone has similar fluency levels in Hindi), Rao decided to have some fun. He stood up and began a memorable speech in Telugu. The gist of it was something like this: 'You are a silly bunch, are you not? At best, you are as smart as straw, which is to say your intelligence is like that of a corpse.' He continued in this vein, enjoying decimating his classmates, secure in the belief that the master could not understand Telugu.

Several minutes later, Rao finished and sat down. Pandit-ji then strode to the front of the classroom and proceeded to translate Rao's invective into Hindi. Much to Rao's embarrassment, Pandit-ji ended by saying he knew a bit of Telugu!

The class erupted in laughter, and Rao was red-faced but forced to smile. His stellar academic record got him a free pass that day, and he did not pay for his cheekiness.

While the son was spending his time at school in the city and frolicking in rivers and soaking up the country life from time to time, the father's political career was steadily progressing. Even though J.V. Narsing Rao had practised law for some sixteen years, it was not to be the career that he would pursue in the long term.

Politics beckoned the lawyer, and he was a stalwart of the Congress party in Andhra Pradesh. By the time he was forty, Narsing Rao had become the president of the Hyderabad Pradesh Congress. As an elected leader, he began to consciously project himself as a flagbearer of unity and justice. These were things he had fought for as a lawyer and perhaps had their roots in the fact that he practised law in a country that was starting to architect itself after having gained independence.

Despite being a part of the traditionally well-to-do Velama community and coming from wealthy antecedents in the Adilabad district in present-day Telangana, the lawyer-turned-politician had, by all accounts, a Gandhian penchant for khadi. And, as Rudyard Kipling memorably said, he had not 'lost the common touch' despite being a person of some standing in society. He retained simple, everyday habits—including chiding his wife for keeping the electric fan on for too long. Not because he could not afford to pay the bills, but because he did not want to be seen abusing his privilege as a public servant by overindulging in using electricity.

Narsing Rao's political journey progressed through twists and turns. His career, in many ways, mirrored that of Telangana, the state that had not been born then. But there was political tension simmering, as people wanted a destiny separate from that of Andhra Pradesh.

Before Independence, the princely state of Hyderabad could be loosely divided into three regions that were linguistically and culturally distinct. The Telugu-speaking Telangana region, which was about half the state, the Marathi-speaking Marathwada region (which became a part of Maharashtra) and a Kannada-speaking Gulbarga region, which went to Karnataka. Apart from this, there was an Urdu-speaking ruling minority. When the British came to India, they signed a treaty with the then Nizam and acquired much of what is today coastal Andhra—areas north of Chennai. Post-Independence, much of the British-held territory was made part of Madras state and the Telangana region part of Hyderabad state. It was only in 1953, after Potti Sriramulu fasted to death for this, that a separate Andhra Pradesh for Telugu speakers was created. In 1956, through the States Reorganisation Act, the Telugu-majority parts of Hyderabad and Andhra Pradesh were merged into a unified Andhra Pradesh; the Marathi-majority areas went to the new Maharashtra state; while Gulbarga, Bidar and other Kannada-majority areas went to Karnataka.

From the early 1950s, the Telugu-majority regions had been fighting for a separate state—Telangana. The States Reorganisation Commission, on whose recommendations the States Reorganisation Act was based, had recommended the creation of a Telangana state. There were a series of protests demanding the creation of Telangana state in 1955–56, but the Andhra Pradesh lobby in Delhi stymied this and kept Andhra Pradesh undivided till 2014.

It is against this political and historical backdrop that Narsing Rao was carving his role. In 1969, Chief Minister Brahmananda Reddy reconstituted his ministry with twenty-nine members. There were eighteen cabinet ministers and eleven ministers. J.V. Narsing Rao was appointed deputy chief minister of Andhra Pradesh. He was given charge of planning, roads, highways, public gardens, city waterworks and matters related to railways and communications.

Rao Sr was a product of both the Benares Hindu University and the Aligarh University—educational institutions that were not only highly ranked but also produced luminaries that ranged from heads of state to top lawyers, athletes and corporate figures.

Narsing Rao undoubtedly made his political entry in the city, but it was in the grassroots and the hinterland where he would carve his legacy. As the chairman of the Andhra Pradesh state electricity board, he brought power to the villages of the state, especially the Telangana provinces.

While he was an important public figure, the frills and benefits of political office did not seem to have mattered to his son and his friends. Politics was never on the agenda. 'My father never wanted us to enter politics. It was taboo for us. For the fifteen years he was a minister, not once did I go to his office,' Nrupender Rao would later write. Why was that so? While neither Rao nor his siblings have a direct answer to that question, it is more than likely that the driving philosophy at the Rao home was to keep the Church (in this case home) separate from the state.

Rao's sister Rekha agrees, saying that their father did not encourage his kids to come visit at work because he wanted to keep his family away from legal and political affairs as much as possible. 'He was protective, especially of the girls, and he did not usually allow them to be around visitors from outside.'

Even as Narsing Rao navigated the choppy waters of Andhra politics, he never lost sight of what mattered to him—home and family. And that included a lifestyle that was far from extravagant.

Life in Hyderabad in the fifties and sixties was casual, laidback and leisurely. Younger people in most households would cycle around or sometimes take the bus. Private cars were not as common as they are today. The food, too, was simple. Rice, upma, dosa, idli and vegetables and dal, usually in the form of sambar, were what appeared on the Raos' table—and indeed on the tables of most Hindu households in the region. North Indian food had not become as ubiquitous as it is today, and even street food like samosas and chola bhaturas were not that easily found. Eating out in restaurants and clubs was something only the business classes and old-money families indulged in.

The young Nrupender Rao grew up watching his father balance the struggle for Telangana, new beginnings and the vicissitudes of public office. As the son of a newly minted minister, the young Rao could have grown up in an atmosphere of privilege and flamboyance, with a sense of entitlement that is often on display with the next generation heirs of modern-day Indian politicians in particular. But Narsing Rao had a strong

Gandhian streak, which was not only seen in his propensity for khadi. His children were brought up minus extravagance. The roadmap for the young Nrupender was not much different from that of any child born into an upwardly aspirational Indian family. There was no room for non-performance. And his father ensured a relentless pursuit of academic excellence.

Rao recalls that after his father's appointment and elevation as a high-ranking official, they moved to a house that was reserved for ministers. 'It was a large house with lawns, fruit trees and attendants. The previous occupant of the house was Laiq Ali, the Prime Minister of Hyderabad, who decided to leave for Pakistan,' Rao recalls. 'I had a room to myself in this house. My siblings and I also had the luxury of going to school in a car, and we stayed in the house for a few years.'

The house in Begumpet was posher than their earlier home. It was cut off from the main city, which meant that the young Rao and his friends would spend more time on a bicycle cruising around from school to each other's homes.

Sometime in 1956, Rao remembers, he wanted to see the offices of All India Radio where his friend Bhushan's father was employed as an assistant engineer. All India Radio's transmitting station was on the outskirts of the city in a lightly forested area called Saroornagar, which was home to smaller animals, including wild rabbits. Managers would shut down the station around 11 p.m.

Rao and Bhushan visited the station, and Rao spent the night at his friend's house. Like in many homes, Bhushan's room had just one electric fan—an Italian Cinni brand table fan. So, after cooking Rao a dinner over firewood and eating in the open air, Bhushan slept in the verandah, leaving his fan-cooled room to his guest.

---

'Baba', as his parents referred to Nrupender, was the first amongst equals when it came to getting the attention of his father, but that did not mean he was spoilt. In fact, the burden of expectation was placed inordinately high, so much so that a basic chiding could have an unexpected impact.

One wintry afternoon in Hyderabad, Rao was summoned by his father and then given a dressing down for a trivial issue that Rao is unable to entirely recollect but feels had something to do with leaving the front door unlocked on the way out to school. Having never been spoken to in that manner by anyone, let alone his father, Rao, teary-eyed, walked straight out of his father's home office and down to the family dining table. On the table was a clay matka, a water pot commonly found in most Indian homes across the country to keep water cool. The teary Rao picked up the matka and began to drink directly from it. He was pouring so much water into his mouth that his mother and sisters became concerned and begged him to stop. The matka held some six litres of water, and they were afraid he would risk physical injury if he gulped that much at one go. 'His stomach might have burst,' his sister remembers with concern.

Rao stopped, and the matter was never discussed again. While Rao cannot remember what the dressing-down was about, one thing is clear—it was not about his academic performance.

---

India has been strongly patriarchal and is only starting to change now. Back when Nrupender was a boy, it was not uncommon for girls to receive poorer education than boys, if they were educated at all. That was not the case in the Rao household. The popular Telugu saying '*Illali chaduvu intiki velugu*' (meaning the woman's education is the light for the entire house) rang true for the way the family saw life. Rao's sisters received as good an education as he did.

Despite being part of a feudal—largely patriarchal—culture, Rao never let his sisters feel he was different from them as far as his role in the family was concerned. Ratnamala, his eldest sister, remembers the time when she was embroidering small flowers on material for a skirt. It was extremely painstaking work, and she was focused on it even as she had a lively conversation with the other sister, Renuka. Suddenly, she remembers, they noticed Nrupender observing them from the corner of the room. They looked inquiringly at him, and he asked: 'How many flowers are you planning to stitch on that?' Renuka laughed. 'Why does it matter to you?' she asked. 'Whether it is one or a hundred, you will never know how to do this!'

Rao smiled at them and did not say more. But one month later, he presented Renuka with a handkerchief on which he had carefully embroidered a motif.

---

One of the reasons people like Narsing Rao were able to focus on their professional careers and on politics was perhaps because business, or the idea of creating an entrepreneurial venture, was then the bastion of the very brave, the very lucky or the very favoured. The few who embarked on ventures belonged to traditionally trading communities like the Marwaris and the Banias, who made the leap to building large houses and industrial organizations. The idea of pursuing business as a vocation in and by itself was not looked upon kindly and was seen as being a necessary evil. The political bedrock of the country had been forged into an unusual combination of self-reliance, or Swadesh, combined with a sharply socialist and sometimes even communist leaning, which was clearly evident in certain states such as Kerala and West Bengal.

Yet, most Indians then, as now, possessed an innate streak that was entrepreneurial. It is no exaggeration that entrepreneurship is as Indian as dal and roti for most Indians. It just takes a few fleeting seconds to realize that under the skin, there is a Dhirubhai Ambani lurking in every thela-wala, roadside vendor, petrol pump attendant and kirana owner. However, back in the fifties, large businesses were seen as out of reach, a distant dream, and very few dared to even join a business, let alone create one. This made it easy for the likes of Narsing Rao to pursue their political and legal lives with dedication and enthusiasm.

Bhushan, who grew up in that era along with Nrupender, says that even as Indians started getting into big businesses post-Independence, a Rs 50 crore turnover was considered huge and commensurate bottom lines were almost seen as sinful. 'Under Pandit Nehru's sense of socialism, it was only the public sector that was seen to be helping the economy and the general state of affairs of the nation. No one looked at an organization's profits, and it would only matter that they were an organized (ethically and morally right) business,' Bhushan says.

What it meant was that big industrially and technologically challenging businesses could only be run by government or quasi-government players and, in a way, that helped create and carve out industries and businesses and supply qualified manpower to generate private enterprises. This included the likes of pharmaceuticals, heavy engineering industries, shipping, hotels, real estate and more.

Of course, there were real and present challenges for any budding business as well. Bhushan says that, for the most part, banks and financial institutions charged anywhere between 20 per cent and 24 per cent in interest on loan of funds to the private sector. There were no non-banking financial companies, organized private equity or venture capital associations in operation then. The remaining choice for a growing business was to be able to stomach such loans at high interest rates, generate robust returns and then pay back that interest and return the capital. So, as a private enterprise, a company had to generate at least 30 per cent in profits in an economy where high margin and high multiples sectors, such as e-commerce, information technology and pharmaceuticals, were either non-existent or in a nascent stage.

In addition, banks at large would pay out 15 per cent in interest rates, which meant they had no choice but to charge high interest rates as well. 'Even a small-time neighbourhood moneylender would charge rates that would border on extortion. They would loan individuals Rs 85 in the morning and demand Rs 100 by nightfall the same day,' Bhushan says with a smile. 'That is how life was then.'

Most were basic industries; profit margins were low and in order to sustain payments and return of capital, all industrialists had to be ingenious, Bhushan opined, adding that expansion meant jugaad, the oft-used Hindi word that is sometimes used interchangeably for innovation but most closely means 'flexible and improvized approaches used to solve existential problems.'

Also, it was not uncommon for several industrial houses to run into teething problems once they started catering to an open and growing India.

Jerry Rao, a native of Bangalore, who ran Citibank in India and even started a technology company called Mphasis, said that shortly after Independence, India had to start making goods for domestic consumption. Its focus, according to him, was to make for India and not for the rest of the world or international markets.

Exports were not the game then; the aim was import substitution, he says. 'India then was, and to some extent even now is, a very poor country; the total non-food GDP of India was comparable to that of Norway's … It was an economy where you could, at the very most, sell around thirty thousand cars in the whole country every year. Crony capitalism did exist in those days, but unlike the other Asian countries which would encourage their inner circles and chaebols to create world-beaters such as Samsung, Hyundai (Korea) or Toyota and Matsushita (Japan), local Indian manufacturers only had incentive to service a market of thirty thousand, using just the automobile industry as an example.'

As a result, such companies would follow the maximum profit strategy. Sadly, the economy then encouraged the emergence of dwarves and pygmies, as manufacturers with very limited markets and growth focus came up, as opposed to global or at least Asian-scale giants that could service countries outside the subcontinent.

The other major challenge for the Indian manufacturing scene was a process called freight (trade) equalization. Railways were nationalized, and it was decided that coal would cost the same in Punjab as it would in Bengal. That led to the setting up of several plants across the country but with diminutive scale. There were other ideas that were decelerating growth, which Jerry Rao says included the way tariffs were set for power. It was designed so that industry should pay more and farmers should pay less and making power the most expensive in the world. Power companies were almost all nationalized, save for Tata Power in Mumbai, which was private.

Hindustan Machine Tools had to set up a factory in Pinjore in Punjab because different political leaders wanted to distribute the manufacturing. That was absurd because there was no raw material or market close by. 'It was like this leader called Manavya KT in the Congress who actually moved the headquarters of ONGC [Oil and Natural Gas Corporation Limited] to Dehradun because he was an MP from Dehradun,' Rao said. The point was to open a business in a place where you could make money.

That was not to say that large companies could not be created in post-Independence India. After all, Tata Steel, which is one of the country's largest corporations and certainly the nation's largest steel-maker, was exactly that. 'However, the Tatas did have a lot of support from the British and then later also the Indian government in setting up and keeping Jamshedpur going,' notes Jerry Rao.

He is not wrong. Named after the founding father of the Tata Group, TISCO or Tata Iron and Steel Company as it was known then, built its plant in 1908, and its first steel ingot was rolled out on 16 February 1912.

At yet another level, a modern India that was led by Pandit Jawaharlal Nehru did not necessarily want to develop much too soon because the concern and fear on the part of Nehru was that a growing legion of communists may have seen the rise as a way of taking power away from the government and thereby controlling votes.

Of course, ultimately, markets cannot be stopped as a force of economic development and growth because they are a function of natural evolution. However, if they are distorted, they can be dangerous because they artificially toy with natural growth, which then makes a country poorer in the long term. Those were the pivotal crossroads that India would be headed towards in the next few decades while politicians and lawmakers were aiming to chart the country's future.

Meanwhile, back in the first couple of decades after Independence, there was what Jerry Rao calls immense negligence when it came to engineering services and hard industries. Core talent went into the civil services and mainstream professions like law and medicine. 'We were not interested in creating legions of engineers. There was a little, but even that engineering progressively became academic and about rote learning.'

In a sense, what he was saying was that India, for all its best intentions, was neglecting the culture and ethos of working with one's hands. Thomas Alva Edison, who invented the electric bulb and the motion picture camera, for example, never went to college and spent most of his time at home being taught by family, reading and experimenting.

That style of tinkering with engineering and working with hardware, says Jerry Rao, was sorely neglected. The result? When Mahatma Gandhi wanted to make his spinning wheel more user-friendly and efficient, he had to go seek out a Polish scholar and engineer named Maurice Frydman, who was living in India at the time because there was no one else with the skills to do the job.

The culture of engineering did not take cues from the Scottish or German traditions and apprenticeships of working in garages and factories and getting one's hands dirty. The country's labour force at that time had hardly created cadres of engineering that could help in practical terms, and the engineers that did exist were vastly more academic than they ought to have been, recalls Jerry Rao. 'The engineers coming out of schools in the sixties were too academic and over time were becoming more and more theoretical and less practical.'

Despite that, engineering was what took the young Nrupender Rao's fancy. By the time he was entering his late teens, India had but a limited number of vocations that students could consider. Medicine, law and engineering sat at the top, with little or no weight given to the arts and the humanities. So, for a younger generation looking to break from the limits of rural India, advanced education was limited to the handful of universities that included the Indian Institute of Technology (IIT), Indian Institute of Management (IIM) and Banaras Hindu University (BHU).

The other option was to go overseas to the Americas or to England, to the halls of the more established centres of learning there. This was immensely difficult. The courses were expensive, sure, plus there was the matter of having sufficient foreign exchange for making payments because the central bank had curbs that were prohibitive. And families that could afford to send their sons abroad to study were reluctant to do so as they were leery of losing their children to a foreign country forever. Rao's uncle, Madhav Rao, intervened and had a heart-to-heart discussion on how the IIT engineering colleges could be an option.

Rao had decided that he could best serve the growing country by becoming a mechanical engineer. Entrance exams to the newly formed IIT had just started a couple of years before Rao was set to take them in 1961. In his typical studious fashion, the young Rao would hit the books for six or seven hours a day, absorbing theories on maths, physics and chemistry and practising high-level exercises and problems in preparation for the exam.

Finally, exam day came, and amidst a lot of nervousness and a little trepidation, Rao sat for it. Weeks later, he got a letter in the mail confirming his admission to the premier engineering school.

For the young man with roots in the Dwaraka village and who had an unshakable reading habit and a boundless appetite for knowledge, the future was unfolding, and it was starting to look bright and wide open.

# 3

# IIT, Indo-Pak Dogfights and an Internship at Godrej

'OH, SO YOU ARE A MADRASI?' RAO BREATHED IN DEEPLY and then exhaled, not knowing whether to laugh or snap that he was not. It was his very first day at college, and he had bumped into Rajiv Tandon, his room-mate to be. 'Where are you from?' Tandon had asked, to which Rao replied, 'I am from Hyderabad.'

Of course, Rao was too polite to show any emotion. Instead, he asked: 'How about you?' Tandon replied, 'Varanasi.' Rao then sat Tandon down and explained to him, step by painstaking step, the various differences between their two cities—their cultures, origins, peculiarities and nuances. After making a casually thoughtless remark, Tandon listened and learned, he said, but it did not matter. The two would go on to become lifelong friends.

In part, the diversity of their backgrounds led to the formation of this unique friendship. 'Remember, there was no TV, no internet and most did not travel widely and deeply across India, so to meet a Southerner or a person from a different state was indeed an experience,' Tandon says.

While the two were as different as chalk and cheese, their pursuit of a higher education was based on the same reasoning and with good cause.

India's first prime minister, Jawaharlal Nehru, envisioned the set-up of a cluster of advanced academic institutes in order to be able to train cadres of skilled technicians to build a country that, he hoped, would become ready to take its place on the global stage. In doing so, he supported the creation of the IITs to provide world-class leaders in technology for an independent India.

The institutions had one primary goal. They were to be equipped with the necessary flexibility of both curriculum and training to be able to adapt in the context of international standards as new frontiers of science and expanding discoveries were being made.

And so, in May 1950, the first of these institutes was created in Kharagpur. The site was the Hijli Detention Camp, a venue where the British had detained prisoners. It was an apt choice: India was liberating minds where its former occupants had imprisoned its countrymen. It was named the 'Indian Institute of Technology' before its formal inauguration on 18 August 1951.

Within a decade of the launch of the first IIT, four more were set up: IIT Bombay (1958), IIT Madras (1959), IIT Kanpur (1959) and IIT Delhi (1961). Decades later, the sixth IIT was established in Guwahati (1994). India's first technical institute, set up in 1847 and known as the Thomson College of Civil Engineering and subsequently the University of Roorkee, was set up as the seventh IIT in September 2001. In the year 2008, six more IITs were born: IIT Bhubaneswar, IIT Gandhinagar, IIT Hyderabad, IIT Patna, IIT Rajasthan, and IIT Ropar. This was followed by two more IITs in 2009: IIT Indore and IIT Mandi. In 2012, Institute of Technology, BHU, was designated the sixteenth IIT. IIT Palakkad and IIT Tirupati came into existence in 2015, and in 2016, five more IITs; IIT (ISM) Dhanbad, IIT Bhilai, IIT Goa, IIT Jammu and IIT Dharwad were started.

Today, it is an established and lofty pursuit to go to an IIT or an IIM, when there is quite literally a world of choice available to a student. But for people like Rao and Tandon, choices were much more limited. For Rao, particularly, the aim was simple: to study in the best place in the country.

Getting into IIT Kharagpur, even for an academically bright young man, meant a lot of hard work. And he was undoubtedly bright. He ranked seventh in the state in his pre-university courses, and eighth in his higher secondary certificate. Because of his double promotion, he was too young for any professional university course. He decided to appear for IIT exams while he was studying in Nizam college for a Bachelor of Science (BSc) degree for that year. 'It was a blessing in disguise as, at that time, I decided that I would seek admission to the prestigious IIT,' Rao says.

Even as he was making academic decisions that would shape his future, Rao was living a bit of a peripatetic existence. His father had started building a house in Gagan Mahal Colony near Domalguda and the family had moved out of the swank ministerial house. They were staying in a house that belonged to one of Narsing Rao's 'followers', close to Gagan Mahal. Once the family moved in, Nrupender Rao took up residence in his room above the garage and began preparation for the IIT entrance exam. He burnt the midnight oil and looked for ways to improve his understanding. One of the subjects he felt he was weak in was engineering drawing. And so he would hop onto his bicycle and visit his friend Vishwas Gadgil's home. Gadgil was a family friend and also a young IIT hopeful and had known Rao since they were teenagers. More important, Gadgil had a tutor who would coach both Rao and him.

After many long months of preparing, it was time to write the entrance exam with thousands of other young hopefuls. Those who knew Rao were unsurprised when he was selected for admission to IIT Kharagpur.

By this time, the family home was completed, and the Raos were all set to move again. For Nrupender Rao, however, this was hardly exciting; he was preparing to move to a new city and make his home there for a few years. One of his father's juniors accompanied him to Kharagpur to help him settle in.

'My dormitory was Azad Hall. The IIT Kharagpur campus was large, and I decided to buy a bicycle so my commute would be easier,' he remembers. The IIT Kharagpur campus was not just large, it was gigantic. Spread over 2,000 acres, it still remains the largest of all IIT campuses.

The mechanical engineering course at IIT Kharagpur was for five years instead of the four years that it is today. For those five years, Rao would have to learn to adjust from living in his father's large house to the collegiate way. 'In my first year, I had to share my room with not one but two room-mates, Rajiv Tandon from Uttar Pradesh and Mandip Kumar from Amritsar,' he recollects. It was only in the second year that they were given their own rooms.

Kharagpur had an air force base but, more significantly, had a railway workshop and a junction—and a sizeable Anglo-Indian population. Back in the day, Kharagpur was intended to be the railway suburb of Midnapore (Medinipur) but had, in time, become an important rail junction. It was replete with workshops and a large railway settlement.

The local industries that kept the place humming along were rice milling, chemicals, steel, shoes and silks. The town was also as secular as it was academic. The city had a Muslim saint's shrine venerated by Muslims and Hindus alike.

Declared a municipality in 1911, it was to become best known for being the cradle of the IITs. But beyond the academics, the railway hub and the workshops, Kharagpur was really little more than a far-flung sleepy town in the middle of nowhere with little to offer by means of social activity. Seen another way, it was perfect for students who were not supposed to be distracted. Rao assimilated there fast and well.

Students on campus used bicycles as the primary mode of transportation. In fact, a cycle was almost an indispensable part of a student's outfit; it was how to go to class, to workshops, and indeed, any form of travel. There was hardly any public transportation available to them. Rao recalls one memorable cycling expedition. 'We once went to Digha, a coastal resort town, which was around 130 kilometres away from Kharagpur. It took us many hours of cycling to reach there,' Rao remembers. Cycling there must have been like participating in a gruelling Tour de France, but once they arrived, the students thought the place was well worth the effort.

Digha had everything that IIT did not. A beach, a waterfront, seafood on sandy stretches—it was all a welcome change from academic confines and mess food. It helped the students reboot their minds. That night, they slept in a small makeshift shack on the beach, and cycled back the next day, tired but refreshed at the same time. 'These were simple pleasures and cost very little but taught students a lot about the value of what life can offer if you just make that effort,' Rao remembers.

There is not a single business leader whose management habits have not been shaped—at least in some part—by their academic environment, and it was no different for Rao. Always confident about making public addresses—no doubt this was something that he had absorbed by watching his father, the politician—Rao jumped at the chance of joining the college debate team, and learned early on in life as he went up against arguments with his closest friends that a different opinion did not mean it was the start of a disagreement. He also learned how to give speeches in style, which meant he remembered facts and figures, and always began or ended a speech or debate with a story, a joke or a quip.

His classmates recall how there was always a quasi-politician lurking in the young man. One summer, Rao stood for election as general secretary and was—for no real reason—simply not doing well in the pre-polling. He then gave a fantastic speech explaining not what he would do but what he would not do, which left everyone spellbound and converted his position from a losing proposition into a winning one, turning the tables on his opponents, Tandon says.

'Unlike many other strong speakers, he left his ego out of debates and discussions and if there was ever a point where matters would become antagonistic, like, say, over North–South divides or India–Pakistan matters and the like, Rao would be sent for by the class because he had the ability to act like a buffer and diffuse the situation,' Tandon said. That skill was to serve Rao well in the years to follow.

At the collegiate elections, Rao went on to support classmate Farooq Mistry, who was part of the same residence unit, Azad Hall, and was going up against Devendra Mishra, who was also in the same class as Rao. Loyalties emanated from the practical common denominator of places of dwelling and not base platforms that included caste, creed or culture.

The music started playing for Rao when Mishra won the elections and became the president of the students' council. 'He was quite an effective president. I was required at my hostel to undertake weekly mess duty,' Rao remembers not very fondly about how he could have happily avoided at least one daily chore. 'One of my tasks was to check the cafeteria supply of milk to ensure that there was no adulteration. To be honest, I did not enjoy my mess duties at all and would have strongly preferred not to do them, but it was what it was. And the takeaway was that life sometimes brings with it banalities that cannot be avoided.'

In due course, Rao was elected as the literary secretary for Azad Hall and later as the general secretary of Azad Hall.

Like many young men his age, Rao, too, encountered a minor crisis that would teach him a long-lasting lesson and, in some ways, shape the future he was heading towards.

It was an accident that every chemistry teacher warns against. One summer, in the middle of a class project in chemistry, Rao was busy taking notes and working through an experiment. He turned to pick up his pencil, which had rolled a little out of reach. As he reached for it, his elbow grazed a beaker full of bromine water. That split second contact was enough for the contents of the beaker to slosh out—on Rao's right hand.

Bromine water is corrosive, and enough had spilled on Rao to burn his hand. He rushed to the college doctor and received preliminary first aid. But he was not convinced that it was enough, so he went into Kharagpur town to consult the doctor there. And he received the news that would have been particularly devastating to a young student.

The Kharagpur doctor examined Rao's hand and said the injuries and the manner in which the damage had occurred would probably hamper easy movement of the hand in future.

This meant Rao could not be a mechanical engineer since it demands some dexterity. The doctor's opinion was based on the premise that in medical injuries, it is not uncommon for contractures to occur when a burn scar matures, thickens and tightens. What then happens is that it can prevent movement, especially if a burn has occurred over a joint.

Rao refused to accept this diagnosis quietly. He declared to the doctor that he would become an engineer, come what may. The doctor, probably used to dealing with hotheaded students, said nothing. He took Rao's injured hand in his and then, without warning, forcibly straightened the fingers that were curled up because of the burn. Rao could not stop screaming. 'It was incredibly painful,' Rao remembers, explaining that what the doctor did caused the skin on his hand to break, leading to even more pain. The doctor merely told him that this was the kind of pain he would have to expect if he wanted to keep using his right hand. He asked Rao to keep exercising his fingers and work through the pain. 'I almost regretted having told him that I would overcome the injury,' says Rao with a reminiscent smile. 'But that was how life went.'

If high school years are an introduction to the adult world, then the college years are the last bastion of youth and, in many ways, a final oasis for those about to become men and women. Like many of his batchmates, Rao could only recall his college years fondly. 'In spite of the rigorous academic schedule, we had a lot of fun at the hostel, and it was not only textbooks as is the common misconception,' he says.

Rao's batchmate, Ravi Kant, adds that 'at IIT, you got in because your grades were top of your class, but that was the last thing that mattered because of the vast number of co-curricular activities as well as the fact that you were thrown into a tank of very smart competitive individuals from diverse backgrounds.'

When IQ levels were more or less the same, then it was really the other character traits that made all the difference at such an institute. Kant himself later went on to work in a host of leadership positions across corporate India, the last and most recent one being managing director and vice chairman of Tata Motors.

But in college, like Rao, Kant and the others enjoyed diversions like films and sports. 'When we were not studying, we would sometimes watch Bengali movies in the IIT auditorium,' Rao says, sharing that even now when he runs into Bengalis in restaurants, malls and elsewhere, he says a line or two from a popular film to break the ice. A top film favourite for Rao and his friends was the Dara Singh–Mumtaz starrer, *Tarzan and King Kong*, produced in 1965—an Indian take on two jungle classics featuring homegrown actors. In due course, Rao found his feet outside of academics, winning table tennis tournaments and receiving recognition for creative writing, notably for an essay called 'If I fell from the IIT Tower.'

Anyone who has lived in a hostel knows that food is of paramount importance. And it was no different for Rao and his friends. 'Every Sunday, we would have Mughlai parathas for breakfast,' he recalls. 'It was a set menu that no one missed because those parathas were just so darned good.'

Tandon, who was Rao's room-mate as well as his best buddy, remembers that the staple fare at IIT included dusty chapatis, watery dal and mostly tasteless food that was not too different from what they probably served at government hospitals or jails. 'By contrast, the Sunday breakfast of Mughlai paratha was without a doubt the best thing to eat. It was made with eggs and dough, crisply cooked with the right condiments and spices and hit the spot every time. The debate was on whether it was stuffed with minced mutton, but the jury was undecided,' says Tandon.

Kant agrees and adds that he has not been able to locate any place outside which can match up to IIT's Mughlai parathas, although he says, a restaurant on Free School Street in Kolkata came close.

Tandon and Rao would often go off with small groups of fellow students on jaunts outside campus to little eateries and snack shops on the fringe. One such fraternity was loosely referred to as the Tuesday Club. One Tuesday, members of this club—Rao, Tandon, a batchmate named Vinod Gupta and a couple of others—headed to Nair's Shack, a place known for authentic South Indian snacks and terrific coffee. At the little snack bar, as they ordered their crisp dosas, they began discussing serious business. They spoke about the need for a students' newspaper to highlight problems that the official paper ignored. And they decided it was time they did something about it. The plan was to start an underground paper called

*Impact* to discuss things that mattered to students—water shortages, the need for improving the campus's infrastructure and other low-level matters.

What the Tuesday Club did not know was that there was a reporter from the widely circulated Kolkata-based *Statesman* newspaper lurking in the background, sipping his coffee and listening to every word. While *Impact* took off and in its early days had more readership than the IIT paper, the *Statesman* reporter wrote a feature on the rebel team that had drafted the idea for *Impact*. Rao, Tandon and the rest were duly summoned into the office of the authorities and were first reprimanded and then told to shut the paper down immediately, recalls Tandon. Then came the carrot. 'Come and revamp the official paper and make it better,' the officials invited them. A couple of them considered this offer and later accepted it. But Rao stood firm to his cause and refused to be a turncoat. 'He was principled like that,' Tandon recalls.

Like almost every college student, Rao learned how to study smart. That involved ripping off their seniors' homework by an innovative process called 'top-oing.' It entailed the following technique. 'One would put a lamp underneath our seniors' work and then place a glass plate on top. The light would shine through the bottom page and the glass, and by placing my own work on top, we could copy the content on the bottom page easily,' Rao remembers with a chuckle and a twinkle in his eye.

College papers and eating out were fun, but when it came down to the serious business of studying, IIT students found themselves in a strange place. They were all class toppers in their various schools. But in IIT, they were with other alpha-type personalities who were almost all over-achievers, driven to excellence and to swim to the top. That also meant that from time to time, winners who were used to only winning would find themselves sinking to the bottom of the class and go through what they had never experienced: defeat, loss and the ignominy of trailing their class. As Tandon says, some students who were valedictorians could not handle coming last or second last, 'but the upside was that there was a kindred spirit and brotherhood that went deeper than any other association any of us had experienced until then.'

That kinship could be seen in the fact that despite the fiercely competitive streak that ran through them all regardless of rank or class, they also all studied together. The best way to actually learn a subject is to go ahead and teach it to someone else, and that is what some of these students would do in little circles with a few classmates sitting around. Every class had a few 'tube lights', the term for slow learners who needed extra help. But the others were open to teaching the rest of the class as it helped them get a leg up on their course work, and yet others had stand out skills that made them most valuable. Pranav Banerjee, recalls Rao, was the best note-taker in the class and 'you could take his writing and repeat it verbatim, and it would make total sense. He was that good.'

There were memorable characters amongst the staff as well. IIT was then one of the few engineering colleges that also had classes in the humanities. There was a history teacher called Kufu Banerjee who was vastly entertaining, well-read and engaging. But he also had a trait that made him laugh nervously after every few lines. Naturally, college students being college students, he was saddled with the nickname of 'He-he Banerjee'. 'Most other teachers who were boring would regularly be heckled but there were some whose levels of expectation tested the students' capabilities to the next level,' recalls Tandon. 'There was a Russian professor who taught engine and machine and design, and he would look at a great rendition and say it is no good; it has to be perfect down to the millimetre.'

In 1965, India and Pakistan went to war. Rao and his batchmates were busy studying, aware of what was going on elsewhere, but not knowing the war would come to them. One morning, Kant recalls, he was shaving when he heard the sounds of two warplanes battling in the skies. He looked out of the window and saw them, unable to believe that he was watching a slice of history from the front row. Nehru Hall, where Kant stayed, was the farthest out and thus closest to the scene of the aerial fight. Kant put his razor down and watched, transfixed. One sortie of Pakistani planes bombarded the Kalaikunda Air Force Base, and then Indian planes responded. It went back and forth and then, finally, a PAF (Pakistani Air Force) Sabre plane was shot down by an Indian Gnat fighter jet.

Rao, Kant and a handful of others scrambled to get on their bikes and rush down to the site of the crash, which was around two kilometres away. What awaited them was a gruesome sight.

The destroyed plane was on the ground while one dead pilot's body had been partially amputated and flung onto a nearby tree, where he hung like a macabre scarecrow. The other pilot lay dead in the plane's cockpit.

Those present picked up little pieces of shrapnel as souvenirs from a war scene but were made to later return it under duress from faculty who had no doubt received a visit from officials at the Indian Air Force. 'At that age, you are excited and thinking of the possibilities of what would happen if the plane came for you or bombed the building that you were in. You think it is a few kilometres away and is not going to impact you,' Kant says.

Like him, Rao too was of the opinion that a souvenir would have been a memento worth cherishing but carrying any aeroplane parts was strictly prohibited, and that wish was soon put to an end, and the students summarily sent back to their respective halls and classrooms.

Even as history was being made around them, the more mundane matters of getting an education had to take precedence. As part of the curriculum, all IIT students had to undergo field training for two years—or rather, two summers of the school year. For the first year, Rao underwent training at Praga Tools in Hyderabad, a company that made machine tools. His work was on metrology and the manufacture of railway couplings, and it being in Hyderabad, made life easy for Rao. 'I stayed at home and commuted to the Praga Tools manufacturing plant, where I observed the making of couplings for railway wagons, which are used to connect rolling stock in a train along with other metrology-related products,' Rao remembers.

Railway couplings are forged first and then machined further. His training began in the metrology shop, where amongst many things, he would learn to roll up his sleeves, dirty his hands and use instruments such as a surface plate, a screw gauge and other equipment. The set-up was both elaborate and engaging, as it involved multiple stages. More important, Rao's internship with Praga Tools showed him that there was a real world outside the universe of textbooks. And, he found, the world outside was far from perfect.

Tandon remembers that in their fourth year, IIT-ians would go to the Hindustan Motors (HM) factory's press shop where metal was being worked upon. Once, a student asked a question about the rejection rates of bumpers (fenders) that were being made. Apparently, the rate was because of a perforation in the middle of the bumper. So, why was there a perforation, asked the student. Nobody knew. So, the company checked with the engineers and they in turn checked with the engineers at Morris's factories and were told that it was used for handbraking mechanical parts which was, of course, not being done anymore and that then saved the HM team a lot of returned fenders.

Earlier, in their third year, Rao and company joined an internship at the Godrej Group. Tandon remembers that they would get in every morning and skip out by lunchtime. The whole plan was to explore Bombay, as it was then called.

Of course, they would do the internship, but they wanted to ensure there was room for adventure and exploration, which was mostly done during the lunch break. Six or seven IIT-ians in their third year went to Mumbai for the internship that lasted six weeks.

Tandon's uncle was director of PR at the Western Railways and had all kinds of contacts at film studios because they were always using trains for film production. The high point was aiming to get access to film studios thanks to Tandon's uncle.

Even as entertainment was the order of the day, the students knew they were there to learn—to understand the workings of Godrej's Vikhroli factory, where the company was then making white household goods that included cupboards, typewriters, forklifts, metal almirahs and refrigerators.

Rao and Tandon stayed at a hostel at Podar College in the city centre. Breakfast would be at a local Irani café, the kind which dotted the city, and were known for their outstanding masala omelettes with fluffy buns, served with piping hot cups of sweetened tea, all at affordable prices even for students. The two would then hop onto a local train that took them to Vikhroli.

At Godrej, the interns would shuttle from department to department and watch products being made from scratch. All that they saw would go into their reports. That was followed by an employee lunch at Godrej's canteen for twenty-five paise and then back to Mumbai, where they would wander around, have dinner at local eateries, and then turn in for the evening. 'The [low] cost of the lunch kept us there for the afternoon;

otherwise, we would have left earlier,' says Tandon, laughing about his student days.

Rao says that either way, they learnt a fair bit from the whole trip to Mumbai. 'After the internship, we had to get back to IIT, and we decided to travel by train from Bombay to Kharagpur. The train was late, and we had to change the schedule. The delay with the new schedule was close to five hours at Jharsuguda, Orissa, which would later become a major industrial hub for metallurgical plants,' he says. 'Since we had a lot of time to spend there, we saw a movie at a local theatre.' The movie was *Shola Aur Shabnam*, starring Dharmendra. They stayed at the train station, and the next day hopped onto an un-serviced carriage and went on to Kharagpur. The movie was about how a struggling young man faces a difficult choice: He is offered a job by his friend, whom he later discovers has gotten engaged to his childhood sweetheart. For young students on their way into the real world, it was a reminder that experiences out there were likely to be bitter-sweet.

# 4

# There Are No Holy Cows in America

On a lazy Sunday afternoon, Yoshihiro Goto, Rao's Japanese room-mate, sipped on Coca-Cola as the muggy Ohio heat percolated into the room. As a thin layer of condensation gathered on the chilled bottle in his hand, Goto looked across at Rao and asked: 'So … how many people do you have in India?'

They were sitting in a two-bedroom apartment in Patterson Heights in Dayton, a small town in Western Ohio. Apart from being the birthplace of Orville Wright, the first man to fly, the town was also strongly associated with aviation and housed the American Air Force's national museum.

The apartment was sparsely furnished with a largeish three-seater sofa and two matching armchairs in green, a couple of side tables, and a few table lamps. One table had a little statuette—an award for best speaker of the evening given by the Toastmasters Club to Rao. On one side of the wall was a book rack that held a few dozen titles and on another was an LP with several records. The only adornment on the wall was a small, coloured sketch of a flower with Japanese inscriptions above it. The window gave the residents of the ground floor apartment a view of the parking lot.

Rao looked at Goto and considered his reply. He put down the small cup of Japanese sencha tea he was drinking and took a deep breath. 'Goto san, we probably have around 500 million people, I think.'

There was silence. Rao was thinking to himself: '500 million people but not enough jobs, not enough clothing, not enough shelter and in many ways not enough solutions for the myriad problems that we have.'

He thought about how India was the largest English-speaking nation in the world even then, despite the English speakers not being the most proficient. If one asked a slightly complex or technical question to an average English-speaking person, it became hard to get an adequate response. Effectively, what that meant was that a company would have to interview a hundred people before they selected one or two candidates as opposed to maybe a dozen people in an English-proficient nation. It also meant more time spent in interviews and the selection process than normal, and the takeaway was that much had to be done to transform the levels of education and communication skills needed to propel India to the top of the development pecking order.

All that went through Rao's head as he answered. His Japanese room-mate, however, saw the statistic in a very different way. Goto jumped up with a gleam in his eye and exclaimed, 'Japan has only 100 million, and you have 500 million! Oh, you are a wonderful country. What an opportunity. My God, if we had 500 million Japanese, we could be the ultimate superpower in the world.'

Rao's thoughts hit the brakes hard and did a mental U-turn. For the first time in his life, he saw that having a large population in a country could be an advantage. Goto's point was that people inherently added value to a nation and when a country had many of them, it was an asset, not a liability, as long as they were skilled, educated and vocationally trained in a disciplined manner. Rao reflected on some of the questions that he used to be asked as a college student at Purdue.

'Oh, India! All those tigers and snakes and elephants, but you speak such good English. How come?' The average American thought that if everybody spoke good English like he did, then India must be a great country. Rao would stand to correct the presumptions. 'No, no, everybody does not speak as well as I do, but there are a lot of intelligent people, but for various reasons, we are continuing to be poor.'

Some months before Goto asked him the question that changed the way Rao thought, he had graduated from Purdue and had joined the working ranks of the American technocracy that was reshaping the country.

His voyage to America happened a few years before that. It was typical in that it mimicked many immigrants from India who had spent their years after school getting advanced technical degrees and then looked to the West in search of qualifications that would augment their skills and allow them to segue into the working world there.

Rao knew early on that he would want to pursue higher education after he graduated from IIT. His father acquired two degrees, and as a mechanical engineer who had trained at IIT, he was of the opinion that an additional degree from a foreign university would round off his Indian education. At another level, he was as keen as any well-educated and adventurous young man to give himself exposure to a more evolved and progressive economic country, namely America.

It was a notion that his parents supported and encouraged but with the understanding that once he graduated, he would return to the mother country. And so, Rao began the process of applying to foreign institutions and colleges. The choice he made was one that threw light on how he was going about his process of selection.

While most might have aspired to reach the hallowed halls of Ivy League universities like Harvard, Yale or Stanford, Rao applied to Purdue University in Indiana. While Purdue, founded in 1869, is self-described as a vast 'laboratory for discovery,' the university was not just known for its science, technology, engineering and math programmes. It was, however, a place where education-seekers came to make their discoveries leading to scientific, technological, social or humanitarian impact.

The university was funded by a land-grant and designed to provide the best possible education to the widest possible audience of students. And thus, it was driven by a mission that was hard-wired to be different from most others. This was the university Rao wanted to graduate from. So, in 1966, after graduating from IIT, Rao began his master's degree in Industrial Engineering and Operations Research at Purdue University.

As is the case with all students going abroad for the first time, Rao's journey was prefaced by excitement, a little trepidation about being alone in a foreign country by himself, all laced with copious free advice from his sisters, parents, cousins and friends.

He flew to America with a layover in Europe. 'We travelled from the old Begumpet airport to Bombay and then on to Paris, France, and were received in Paris by a friend,' Rao recalls. Paris, that dream of tourists everywhere, had plenty of attractions for Rao. And because Paris was just a hop, skip and jump away from London, Rao went there too. He visited friends and family, as well as a couple of Indian restaurants, before getting on the flight to Chicago. In Chicago, he was joined by his cousin, Upender Rao, who came from Milwaukee, Wisconsin, to meet him.

The great Indian social network, which swings into action when countrymen travel abroad, works like magic every single time, even if it is notoriously inefficient when everyone is back on the subcontinent. Rao and his cousin hopped on to a small plane for a short-haul flight to Purdue in West Lafayette, where he was given room and board at a transit house. Later, he switched to a boarding house where some other Indian students were also staying for a year.

Rao's room-mate at the house was a student named Jagdish Bihani. Having been accustomed to home-cooked, Indian food for most of his life (even at Kharagpur, while the food was certainly not home-cooked, it was Indian), it took some doing for Rao to get used to the university cafeteria. It was a predominantly meat-based menu—the standard American offerings of burgers, pizzas, grills, roasts and sandwiches—but that was not an issue for Rao. What took him aback was the fact that the meat was beef—the one meat Hindus do not eat, as they consider the cow sacred. Rao discovered that there was beef in the tacos, beef in the burgers, beef in the marinara sauce, beef in the sandwiches and even beef for breakfast.

The alternative to beef was bland and vegetarian, and Rao could not stomach that. A couple of weeks of misery trying to find palatable food led to a memorable conversation with some of the others in his boarding house. 'American cows are not the same as Indian Hindu holy cows, and therefore you can eat them. It is as simple as that,' he was told. Rao was happy to buy that argument.

Rao's time at Purdue flew by in a flash as he absorbed the way in which the West worked, learnt to integrate with them and even allowed it flexibility to creep into his dietary preferences, and indulged in the occasional burger.

Every evening after dinner, Rao went to the library to study for a few hours and went into hyper-mode to finish up his courses. In a single year, he completed coursework for three semesters as he also took summer courses. When he finally did graduate, the young man was mainly thrilled about being able to wear his graduation gown. It was a first and a special feeling because he had missed attending his IIT convocation due to travel constraints.

Rao applied to a bunch of companies and finally received a job offer from National Cash Register (NCR) in Dayton, Ohio. His major in college was Operations Research, and that was what NCR was looking for at the time. NCR began as the National Manufacturing Company of Dayton, Ohio, and went on to make and sell the first mechanical cash register. The cash register was invented in 1879, and five years later, the company and patents, both, were bought by John Henry Patterson and his brother Frank Jefferson Patterson. The new firm was renamed the National Cash Register Company.

The company went on to go public, acquire many other ventures and even do top secret work for the government—crypto-analytic equipment, high-speed communications and code-breaking. Later, it would go on to make small computers and eventually get acquired by AT&T Communications.

As an industrial engineer at NCR, Rao would work on a project to automate and integrate cash registers with inventory management systems for food supply businesses.

All the while, at the back of his mind, there remained the quest for more advanced education and training. In truth, his interest lay in higher education, and he gained admission to PhD programmes at top-ranked institutions—Columbia University and Stanford University.

Rao would eat lunch at NCR's office and have dinner at his cousin Vala Dharamsagar's place. 'We took turns cooking dinner. However, I was not a particularly good cook, so I was often allowed to miss my turn,' Rao reminisces, with a glimmer of mischief in his eye. On weekends, Rao would drive over to Cincinnati, which was close to Dayton, and catch up with his friend Boka Sudarshan Reddy, who, Rao remembers, was a particularly good cook.

Of course, Cincinnati was also a larger, more exciting city, famous for its sports teams, theatre, orchestra and ballet shows. Cincinnati also had the historical distinction of being home to the first baseball team in America: the Cincinnati Reds. So, Rao did what any smart immigrant would do—work hard during the week and head to the city for fun and adventure during the weekend. 'On one trip, we forgot our apartment keys in Cincinnati and had to turn all the way back to get them,' Rao recalls, laughing.

One winter evening on a Sunday in Dayton, the phone rang. Rao, who was reading *Words* by Jean-Paul Sartre, jumped off the couch and turned down the record player, which was blaring a vibrant tune by trumpeters Herb Alpert and the Tijuana Brass, before he answered the phone. It was his college buddy, Tandon, who was also in the USA, working there. 'Is this Nuni Rao?' asked the voice. 'Who wants to know?' shot back the receiver of the call before erupting into a laugh. Back in 1965, when Rao and Tandon were at IIT, the nickname that he had gotten was Nuni because the local folks just could not get to learn how to pronounce his name correctly.

Rao was no less. He came back at Tandon and asked him how life in 'Oo-tah' was, intentionally pronouncing it wrongly to get a rise out of his friend. Tandon kept quiet and then corrected him the second time, and explained that it was pronounced You-Tah, not Oo-tah, and Rao feigned ignorance and then said it wrong again later.

In 1967, Rao and a few of his friends and cousins decided to visit Montreal to attend Expo 67, one of the largest events held to mark Canada's centenary. The theme of the expo was 'Man and His World' and was located on 400 hectares of man-made islands in the St Lawrence River adjacent to Montreal.

The event promised to be a feast to the senses of curious intellectual immigrants seeking to expand their horizons and deepen their knowledge of the world. Inspired, the friends packed their bags and hit the Canadian roads in an Oldsmobile Vista Cruiser station wagon and a Buick.

Rao was a shutterbug, and for people like him, travel presented innumerable opportunities. The road trip proved to be a godsend for the aspiring lensman with an eye for scenic vistas and unusual moments. 'I got my first camera when I was thirteen years old, and it was a hobby that never left me,' Rao says. Later, when he moved to Dayton, his Japanese room-mate assisted him in taking his passion to the next level. Yoshihiro Goto helped him buy a Japanese camera with wide angle and telephoto lenses and Rao began to shoot several photos during his trips, later even buying a more sophisticated professional Nikon camera.

'Our first stop in Canada was in Ottawa, the capital city. We visited the Thousand Islands National Park and then travelled to Montreal, saw the expo and then returned to the US via Maine and Vermont,' Rao remembers. 'Then, we visited Niagara Falls and then returned to Ohio.'

Rao got hooked by the travelling bug, and all his holidays from then on went in Route-66 style road trips of the country when holidays came. The Canada road trip inspired the friends to repeat the experience in the USA.

'Our Tour of America started with Kansas and continued through Arizona, where we saw the Grand Falls close to Flagstaff. We then travelled to California to the city of San Diego. We visited an open zoo there and then went to San Francisco and saw the famous Lombard Street (the crookedest street in the world) followed up with a visit to Lake Tahoe, a freshwater lake,' says Rao, remembering every detail of that trip.

That was followed by a visit to Yellowstone National Park in Wyoming, world-famous for its geysers and hot springs. Old Faithful is one of the most famous geysers and erupts every hour or so. Rao was fascinated with the country's natural heritage, which he found was as unique as it was beautiful. It reminded him in some ways of India with its range and diversity that included the fertile farmlands of the Punjab on the one hand and the vast desert-wrapped sand dunes of Rajasthan on the other, and everything else in between.

One memorable moment that stayed with him, especially because he was lucky enough to capture it on film, was when he was in Yellowstone. The car in front of him, loaded with an American family on vacation, suddenly slowed down, causing them to decelerate.

They looked to their right, and then they saw why. A large, full-grown brown grizzly bear was ambling across to their car. The bear walked to the car and stood on two legs, almost human-like, as it peered through the front window at the car's driver. The moment froze in time as everyone wondered what would transpire next; Rao, though, pulled out his camera and got a memorable shot. The bear then dropped back down on all fours and scooted off back to the wilds, satisfied it was not missing out on something.

The journeying continued. From Wyoming, they went to Keystone, South Dakota, and visited Mount Rushmore. Rao checked off an imaginary box in his head; the massive carvings of American presidents were something he had only seen in *Life* and *Time* magazines.

Next came Reno, Nevada, which—like Las Vegas—was full of casinos and the promise of getting rich quick. Rao did not fall for that and always remained a spectator.

The last few cities on the list included a horse farm in Kentucky, and the final halt in Oklahoma City. 'This capped off our American tour, and I had a great time visiting so many cities with such rich history and culture,' says Rao. The drive back to Dayton was over hundreds of miles, through mountain ranges and straight roads, which the friends navigated comfortably to the tune of soft country and rock music that played on the radio stations.

Even as Rao was soaking in the American lifestyle, working long hours and equally taking tons of outdoor trips and seeing what America was all about, his parents—through letters and occasional telephone calls—made it abundantly clear where his long-term future was—back in India.

Rao was conflicted, knowing that there was so much more that he wanted to learn and achieve while in America. He wanted to get a doctorate from an Ivy League school and had even got admission at some, but there was no green light from home in Hyderabad.

Hoping he could talk his father out of having to return, Rao wrote the minister a letter and explained that there was a real and serious shortage of jobs in the subcontinent for engineers like him with advanced degrees, and even if there were jobs, it was unlikely they would offer substantial compensation compared to what he had gotten used to.

The truth was, of course, that the notion of attending a doctoral programme at either Columbia or Stanford University, where he had already gotten admission was starting to gnaw away at him.

His father, however, was very clear that he wanted his son back in India. It is worth noting that not only did J.V.N. Rao grow up at a time when primogeniture was the norm, but he also perhaps saw immense potential in his son being able to perform in an India that was headed towards transformation.

Most likely, the concern was—as in the case of the many Indian parents who send their children abroad—that Rao would get married to an American and settle down there, never to return.

Either way, having been raised in a family with strict Gandhian ideals, Rao eventually found it difficult to go against his father's wishes but used the scarcity of good jobs as an excuse that his father acted upon by arranging an interview with Coromandel Fertilisers, that then had a partnership with Amoco of USA. The Amoco Corporation was an American chemical and oil company founded in 1889, around a refinery located in Whiting, Indiana. When the day for his interview came with the executives at Amoco, instead of prepping and reading up and being ahead of the curve, Rao took it easy. He said what he thought and never once made an effort to impress or please the man quizzing him. In fact, at various points in time, he even tried to be a contrarian and dispute common wisdom when it came to Amoco and business in India.

If he thought he had succeeded in stymying his own chances at getting a job with Coromandel and ensuring his stay in America, Rao was dead wrong. The Amoco executive highly recommended him as someone who 'has his own mind and is not afraid of arguing … with strong convictions … qualities which form an important part of leadership.' He got the job, his fate was sealed, and his return to the motherland was imminent.

Knowing that he would not be able to travel as freely once back in India, Rao decided on a last hurrah. He booked a flight to India via Europe. He stopped over in Europe and took in well over half a dozen countries. He visited Frankfurt and Berlin in Germany, Copenhagen in Denmark, Stockholm in Sweden, Rome in Italy, as well as cities in Austria, Greece and Egypt. How did he manage to afford it all? In part, his frugal Indian habits kept him chugging along, and for the rest, he picked up tips from a handy little title by Arthur Frommer called *Europe on 5 Dollars a Day.* Frommer was like a one-man version of today's *Lonely Planet* guides that give travellers tips on everything from hotel, travel, food and sight-seeing when on the road.

Rao travelled by subway trains and stayed in homes for paying guests as he traversed Europe. Compared to America, which was a nation that was new and being built ground up, Europe was a sharp contrast. In Europe, he saw modern buildings and wide roads as well as antique and historical buildings. He visited the Parthenon in Greece. In Austria, he attended an opera. In Germany, he visited Bad Reichenhall, noted for its famous orchestra and spas, but missed Salzburg. The last leg of his trip was a visit to Egypt. The pyramids and the Sphinx fascinated the homeward bound man, and then, in an almost Shakespearean omen that seemed to want to keep Rao from going back, there was a sandstorm in Egypt at the time of his flight which was consequently delayed.

At the airport, as he reflected on his time spent in America and his many experiences, his room-mate Goto's words started to sink in about the inherent advantage that India had because of its number of people.

Rao reflected back on how the Indian spiritual leader Swami Vivekananda had, during a visit to Chicago, said: 'We cannot think of being an economic power and being only in-and-in.' Swami Vivekananda had years earlier gone to Chicago and talked about his concept of 'Vasudaiva Kutumbakam', which in essence theorized that the world was one large family, truth was the only god, and one's country was the whole world. Globalization, in other words, was only driving that theory to truth. Rao did not know it then, but globalization was the very business phenomenon that was to sweep the world in the next few decades.

Meanwhile, many economic changes were also sweeping through India, and Rao would go on to talk about them much later in India. 'When we were free, we were afraid of being slaves, so we went by the socialist model, the socialistic pattern of society, which is what Pandit Jawaharlal Nehru propounded. He was influenced by Fabian Socialism of 1935 that went on for a while,' says Rao, explaining the economic backdrop to the India he had returned to. After a while, those in power saw that it was not working, so by around 1990, they decided to grow further on the twin planks of liberalization and globalization.

'Liberalization meant, make India free for all Indians. License, quota, permits—let us eliminate it, let us reduce it. The second is globalize. Indians are free to export their products all over the world,' Rao would find himself proclaiming many years later.

His speech came late, but the seeds of the thoughts were present since he was in America. He would often reflect on how the joke was that for companies in the subcontinent, there were always two categories when it came to quality: Indian and 'export quality'. 'So what was not sent off for export was pushed right back into the Indian market.'

It did not work like that in countries that were ahead of India on the industrialization curve. Rao went to Japan on a business visit when working for NCR because they supplied a machine made by their counterpart in Japan. 'I went to Kobe, and they said they have a slogan that whatever is good … whatever is of the right quality and the right standard, it goes to Japan, and whatever is not that great then goes to export. It was the exact opposite of what India was doing, which was what was good went to export, and what was not good was served up to the Indian people.'

The point was that Japan had set a benchmark for its products on quality despite making the best for themselves, and that meant that if you wanted to truly excel at quality as a manufacturer, then one would have to produce one's very best at home and then ship off the rest to the world.

By the sixties, India was moving towards standing on its own feet and becoming economically independent but was nowhere near the levels of advancement that were to come with real liberalization in the nineties. Liberalization opened up the markets from the inside and also to the world outside. In other words, it was in the nascent stage of almost everything. How many indigenous automobile companies of scale existed?

One or maybe two. The number of large national hotel chains? Maybe one or two. Commercial airliners? One. America, meanwhile, had dozens of hotel chains that included Howard Johnson's, Holiday Inns, Hilton, Best Western, Sheraton, Ramada, Hyatt, Travelodge, InterContinental and more. Airlines included TWA, Aloha Airlines and Pan Am.

At a deeper cultural level, America in the sixties was a land of rebellion, mini-skirts, the Beatles, the counter-culture movement of Haight-Ashbury and the advent of women's lib, while India, still in its third decade of freedom after the ejection of British colonialists, was grappling with Licence Raj, prohibition, severe economic controls and equally severe shortages of natural resources.

After a year in Dayton, and his grand tour of Europe, Rao was finally ready to get back to India. As his flight was called and he boarded his aircraft, he thought about the multiple tautology possibilities his country would hold for him now that he was heading back. Of course, he was also keenly aware that while he had been equipped with a new set of skills, the real change that had been affected was in his mind. Rao was no longer just an engineer with an advanced degree. He was now hardwired to see the world as a technologist would. He knew how theory worked and had seen how it could be implemented in the Western world. He did not know it then, but his new job in India was only going to be a stepping stone towards that end.

# 5

# A Passage to India, New Beginnings and an Unexpected Departure

For an immigrant, coming back from America to India can mean two things. One is that the trip to the West did not result in success. The other is that the immigrant came back home because of circumstances that left no other choice but to bid farewell to the land of the free and the home of the brave.

For Rao, of course, it was neither of the above. He was back home because his family wanted him to be there and while he may not have known it at the time, his parents obviously had charted out life plans that went beyond his profession and job, although that was what he first jumped right into.

Coromandel Fertilisers is today owned by the low-key, family-owned Murugappa Group. The company is called Coromandel International and is India's second-largest phosphatic fertilizer player. Back when Rao joined, the company was into fertilizers, speciality nutrients, crop protection and retail.

It had American roots; Coromandel Fertilisers was incorporated in 1961, thanks to the efforts of two large American corporations—Chevron Chemical Company and International Minerals and Chemicals Corporation, in conjunction with East India Distilleries and Sugar Factories, better known as EID. (EID was closely associated with Parry & Company, a sugar, ceramics and engineering goods company, and in 1975, was incorporated as EID Parry.)

In 1968, when he came back to Hyderabad, Rao had the advantage of having a job even before he got off his aircraft. So, he cruised seamlessly into a management position at Coromandel. However, by his own admission, it did play out in his mind that he had, at least in some part, gotten the job as a result of a reference made by his father. That fact, combined with the parallel reality that he was not very incentivized by the work he was getting to do after National Cash Register (NCR), led him to slowly and surely start to get disinterested and bored with his role. He later said that he 'did not have enough work' and started scouting around for other opportunities. The truth was plain and simple: he did not like the gig at Coromandel.

His stint at Coromandel lasted for less than a year. Given his advanced qualifications and the limited number of large multinationals in the vicinity, his choices were not too plentiful. He ended up interviewing with Union Carbide in Madras (now Chennai). At the time, the foreign-owned

Union Carbide—which kicked off its India business in 1934—employed close to 10,000 people and made a range of products from batteries to plastics, pesticides and marine products. Rao was a natural fit, given his prior experience and training, and was promptly hired.

'I was interviewed by Union Carbide at Madras. The interviewer was American, and the works manager was a Britisher named Alan Feaver. The head of Industrial Engineering at Union Carbide was K.V.K. Raju. He gave me a test which I cleared with ease. I was also interviewed by the works manager and the plant head, and I remember answering, and them being satisfied with my answers,' Rao recalls.

The best part of it all: they offered him a job at twice his current salary.

There was no reason for Rao to refuse. As soon as he signed on, he was sent to Calcutta for training, and once he completed that, he joined Union Carbide's Madras office.

K.V.K. Raju, the other executive who was watching Rao, was soon promoted and transferred to Hyderabad, but their paths were to converge in the near future.

Even while Rao was seizing career opportunities, his horoscope had already been sent around, and a suitable life partner had been selected by his parents. That was, in all likelihood, the other key reason his parents wanted him back from the USA. And so, on 7 May 1970, Rao married Rajyalakshmi, the daughter of Inuganti Chinna Rao of Samarlakota in the East Godavari district. Samarlakota was known as a holy town, with a number of temples built in honour of Lord Shiva, the destroyer in the holy trinity where Brahma is the creator and Vishnu the preserver. Hers was also an illustrious family; her great-grandfather, Raja Rama Rayanam, built the famous Satyanarayana Swami temple at Annavaram. That temple is now run by the state government. The temple is part of a trio of religious monuments that includes the Kanaka Durga temple in Vijayawada and the Laxmi Narasimha Swamy temple in Visakhapatnam, believed to be second only to the Tirupati temple in terms of power and sanctity.

The wedding ceremonies were conducted, as is customary, at Samarlakota, the bride's ancestral home. The reception, however, was in Hyderabad at the Exhibition Grounds, one of the spaces large enough to accommodate the hundreds of guests.

Even as the guests flowed into Exhibition Grounds, Rao's childhood memories of the place came flooding in. Aside from political office, his father had been the president of the Exhibition Organization Committee, and as a child, Rao had visited many of the stalls and learned from them. He and his siblings had spent several summers there as they would eat, shop and ride the merry-go-rounds, and meet most of their friends and social peer groups there. He was aware that his youth was ending as his life entered a phase where he would now assume the role of a husband, a provider, and later, a father.

Soon after his marriage, Rao and his wife flew to Delhi for their honeymoon, where they stayed at the guest house maintained by the state of Andhra Pradesh. Then they flew to Srinagar in Kashmir, a popular wedding and holiday destination. The young couple did what most newlyweds in India did in those days: rent a houseboat and go for a ride on a shikara.

That was followed by a trip to Gulmarg and then onward to Pahalgam. 'We drove back to Srinagar afterwards and then flew to Delhi and back to Hyderabad. We had the opportunity to see Birla Mandir and the Qutub Minar,' recalls Rao. It was the first of many trips he would take with family.

But that was still to come. Standing at his wedding reception, greeting guests, Rao thought about how great life was turning out to be. He began softly whistling the tune of a song 'What a wonderful world' by popular jazz musician Louis Armstrong:

> I see skies of blue and clouds of white
> The bright blessed day, the dark sacred night
> And I think to myself, what a wonderful world

Rao had indeed got a lot to be thankful for. His career was on track and he was home on his own turf and had started a family, with the tacit backing of his family and relatives in everything he did.

His wedding and honeymoon done and complete, Rao went back to Chennai, where he dove into work and got busy with his role at Union Carbide.

After a few months, he was relocated to Hyderabad, where he worked as an industrial engineer; 'I did attempt to educate myself on several other job profiles,' says Rao, but his engineering background was too valuable for the company to ignore. K.V.K. Raju, who had been the head of Industrial

Engineering at Union Carbide's Chennai outfit and was instrumental in hiring Rao, had been promoted to head the Hyderabad division.

When Rao started working at the Hyderabad factory, a Mr Gokhale was the works manager. He was soon replaced by Subroto Bose. The industrial relations manager was a gentleman called Mr Mudiraj, who was said to be biased in favour of unionized workers. As often happens in factories with unions, there was a lot of politics, and Mudiraj resigned. The company decided to appoint an assistant industrial relations manager. Raju persuaded Bose to try Rao in that role.

It was Rao's first experience with industrial and labour relations and his experiences there framed and shaped his views on how to create, ensure and maintain cordial ties between a well-aligned union and the management.

As with any union-related job, Rao faced several trials by fire. He had to deal with that nightmare peculiar to factory owners and management—the workers called for a strike. It was on the verge of getting violent, with the union physically preventing staff members from leaving the factory grounds. For the first time at work, Rao became tense.

He reached out to Nirmal Bose, an advisor with Union Carbide at their Kolkata office. Bose gave him some advice that would stay with Rao. It was the best possible advice, the simplest, and also the hardest to follow: Be firm. Bose advised Rao not to buckle or give in, no matter what. He suggested that the management not yield, and announce a lockout the next morning.

The next twelve hours were stressful, but they taught Rao the value of sticking to his guns and staying true to his resolve. By dawn, the union allowed Union Carbide's employees to go back home, and the strike ended on their terms.

On the home front, Rao was soon celebrating the birth of his first child, Arathi, in 1972. She was the first of his three children, and while Rao's parents were already grandparents, they had the joy of welcoming their second granddaughter.

In life, moments of great joy are sometimes served on the same plate as great loss. Within a year of becoming a grandfather, Narsing Rao was contesting the assembly elections of 1972. He won with a huge majority from his constituency of Luxettipet. But he was dissatisfied. He believed that he had not been given the kind of prominence that he was striving for in the corridors of power in Hyderabad. But that looked set to change.

Shortly after the assembly elections, Narsing Rao heard from well-placed sources in the Congress Party that Prime Minister Indira Gandhi was soon going to summon him for a discussion on the state of political affairs in Andhra Pradesh. Before meeting the Prime Minister, the senior Rao decided to fix a troublesome sinus condition that sometimes hindered his speech. It also resulted in headaches, sneezing and stuffiness in his respiratory passages, and coughing spells. It was not a serious problem, but it annoyed him, and he wanted it fixed.

Sometime before this, he had met a surgeon who had told him that surgery could fix his problem. The surgeon told Narsing Rao that it was a fairly routine, quick and painless procedure. The senior Rao decided to go for the surgery, expecting it to ease his public life as it would eliminate the speech problem as well as the headaches and sniffles. He told the surgeon he was ready for surgery.

Topical cocaine was historically favoured by many surgeons for sino-nasal surgery due to its superior vasoconstrictive and anaesthetic properties. Doctors would introduce cocaine packs in the nasal cavities after a procedure to restrict bleeding and pain. This was not a recommended practice if the patient had diabetes or high blood pressure. The senior Rao had none of these problems, and so the surgeon went ahead with using topical cocaine.

The surgery was deemed a success, but Narsing Rao was not sent home due to post-operative bleeding. As a result, he stayed overnight at the hospital. The next morning, the cocaine pack was removed, and as that process was complete, Rao started settling down, but then he complained of a severe headache, which grew worse in no time. The medical help at the hospital gave him painkillers and suggested he eat, which he tried to but could not beyond a spoonful of food. In effect, the pain was so bad that he could not eat. He tried to speak, but all that emerged was a garbled stream of incoherence. His daughter called the doctors, but Rao soon lost consciousness and fell into a coma while he was being examined. He was wheeled into intensive care. His family was told that he suffered a brain haemorrhage.

The neurosurgeon attending to him said it was unlikely that Narsing Rao would survive for more than six or eight hours. The family swung into action. He was put on a heart-lung machine, and word was sent to his eighty-eight-year-old father, Gopal Rao. The old man rushed to the city to be by his son's side. But Narsing Rao seemed determined to prove the doctors wrong, and fought for almost two weeks. However, he gave up the fight on the auspicious Ekadashi day, the third of September.

'The state has lost a fine leader … and I, a valuable friend,' announced P.V. Narasimha Rao, then chief minister of Andhra Pradesh, who went on to become the Prime Minister. It was the end of a generation.

For Nrupender Rao, then all of twenty-seven, life was never the same. His father was no more, and the harsh reality of getting on without him dawned on Rao. For all his public profile and widespread fame, fortune eluded the senior Rao. When he died, he was far from wealthy and was perhaps even a little distanced from the ground realities of life.

His daughter, Rupa, now a doctor herself, residing in the United States, recalls how when her father passed away, they had to hunt high and low to find his life insurance policy and papers. When they found the documents, they realized that he had stopped paying premiums after the second payment, she said. It was not that he was trying to default; it was more like he simply did not think it was too important and forgot about it. Also, he was only fifty-eight and perhaps had not seen the urgency in keeping such an arrangement going. In any case, it left his sons and daughters scrambling to find ways to take care of his last rites, the cremation and all the traditional ceremonies that are expected to be performed when a man dies.

While Rao and his sisters were independent adults, their father still took care of everything that was tied to the home. With him gone, all the duties and family responsibilities not only fell on Rao's shoulders but also took precedence over his career, and so he chose to stay in Hyderabad.

There is a line attributed to Sigmund Freud that says no one can be a man unless his father has died. This is something that Rao thought about a lot in the days following his father's death. He realized how lucky he had been to enjoy the reflected glory that fell on him because of his father's position, status and role in society. As he walked through his father's room, he saw a copy from his own collection of Dale Carnegie's best-seller *How to Win Friends and Influence People*, and he recalled when he had come across the book with his father. His father had seen the book, picked it up and flipped through it. He had smiled and said: 'One could read such books, but one was better served in remembering the sincerity of words and action as opposed to getting wed to elements of manipulation that could become a habit and a way of life.' He remembered how his father had pushed not just him and his siblings into higher education but had convinced even his mother to study more. When her six children reached a certain age, he convinced her to enrol for a master's degree in Telugu at Osmania University. 'While the children went to school and college, my mother was attending university,' Rao smiles at the memory. J.V.N. Rao wanted all his children to be well-travelled and well-read.

Rao's own secular values and principles were directly derived from watching his father whose own education, divided between Aligarh and Banaras, gave him as broad a mind as possible. He was equally comfortable wearing kurta pyjamas as he was in a sherwani and speaking in Urdu.

Rao remembers that one day, a guest complained to his father over dinner that he was perhaps being too kind and showing too much regard to the engineers at the Public Works Department. His father put down his fork and knife and asked the guest if he ought to extend respect to his son sitting at the table, who was then an engineer with two years of experience. 'Of course,' exclaimed the guest, 'with no question.' Then Rao's father asked, 'Why should I treat engineers at the works department, who have as much as three decades of experience, with any less regard?' His point hammered home to all at the table and Rao reminisced how progressive his father actually was, given that he had not travelled, worked or studied outside of India. Standing in his father's room, these memories revolving in his head, he felt a moment of loss and bewilderment. But that left him as he considered the weight of the responsibilities that lay ahead of him.

His sister, Rupa, and brother, Naresh, were not yet married, he needed to have and raise his own children, and his mother and other siblings were going to no doubt look to him for guidance and support. His mind turned towards his career prospects and the possibilities he could entertain now that he had decided he was going to stay on in Hyderabad.

Rao could have shifted gears and joined local politics like his father had and could have moved up the political ladder into the corridors of power. While he did get offers to jump onto the political bandwagon, both his wife and his mother cautioned him against it. Already, the signs of southern politics turning into the blood sport it now is becoming more and more pronounced. Before his father died, passing miscreants who supported the creation of a separate 'Telangana' lobbed a homemade bomb through the window of the family home in Hyderabad. The intensity was low-grade, and no one got hurt, but the message was clear.

Through all this, K.V.K. Raju had become more of a friend and mentor to Rao than just a senior work colleague. It was easy to see why, since the two had much in common.

Like Rao, Raju came from the fertile river basin of Juvvalapalem, West Godavari district, from an agricultural family. Like Rao's father, he too was bred with a strong emphasis on education and graduated from BHU and the Madras Institute of Technology. He went on to get an advanced degree in mechanical and industrial engineering from Michigan State University and the University of Minnesota in America. He worked there for a while but returned to India, where he worked with the likes of Caltex Oil Refinery, Orient General Industries, Associated Electrical Industries, and then Union Carbide of India, where he was for fifteen years. Raju's move into entrepreneurship would eventually serve as a role model for his young friend.

'At the same time Raju had left to start his own company, Union Carbide had considered me for a new role at Kolkata, where a new project was being constructed, but I decided to pass on it,' Rao said. 'I decided to resign and join K.V.K. Raju's new company.' The die had been cast, and that one single career move would change Rao's career, future and work-life prospects forever.

---

Raju had been with Union Carbide for a long while across its major metro offices and was driven by the urge to serve India better by creating jobs and adding value to the economy. In 1973, he started the Hyderabad-based Nagarjuna Steel, which went on to become the precursor for the Nagarjuna Group and which kickstarted ventures in chemicals, fertilizers and more.

Of course, Union Carbide tried hard to prevent two senior engineers from leaving at the same time. 'They [Union Carbide] tried to retain me, and I was called in to Kolkata to meet Dr Bhattacharjee. They heard me out and then what was supposedly a perk, one of the directors arranged for me to see a tennis match,' Rao muses. 'However, I had made my decision and communicated this to them, so they had no choice but to accept my resignation.'

In any case, Rao was never driven by power or the limelight. Having been exposed to industry in America, he was more enthused by the idea of belonging to an organization that was impacting rapid and real change to the nation's economic and business landscape.

Rao then proceeded to join Raju at Nagarjuna Steel in Hyderabad. Ironically, the office was right across the street from Coromandel Fertilisers' office, the place where Rao had first gotten his job when he came back to India from the USA.

It was something of an inspiration for Rao to watch Raju shift from being a big company manager to a self-starting entrepreneur. Back then, India was not entrepreneur-friendly, and the systems of finance were not geared to support smart ideas created by smart men with initiative.

There was no organized venture capital, no private equity outfits, and significant projects were given only to large organizations and companies. Everyone in Rao's IIT batch, for example, ended up working for a big firm. They all then tried for a scholarship to study further in the USA and hoped to find well-paying jobs there. What Raju was doing by eschewing the 'good job' and taking a risk as an entrepreneur was path-breaking.

When Raju started Nagarjuna, his vision was to make it a professionally run firm with well-qualified managers to supervise core functions. He hired R.P. Hasan as its finance chief and a senior Tube Investments employee as the plant manager. Rao was put in charge of human resources, with a specific mandate to onboard all the staff, including the management team. To ensure that worked out to plan and that Nagarjuna had a strong core team, Rao travelled to Bombay, Madras and Rourkela and hired the most experienced workers he could find.

In a world where most Indians were still not used to travelling outside of their home states for long periods of time, it was easier to hire South Indians as they could adapt better to the living and working conditions in Hyderabad. To his surprise, Rao discovered that one of his hires, an engineer from Tube

Investments who had joined Nagarjuna Steel, had left behind bosses who were miffed at his departure.

Apart from the hard business lessons in setting up a corporation and building it block by scrappy block, Rao was also absorbing how vital it was to manage the relationship aspect between partners, vendors and clients.

Raju believed in following a distinct, methodical process for receiving important guests. He personally received them when they arrived in Hyderabad and he went to drop them off when they left. They would be given flower bouquets to welcome them and photos would be taken of their visit and their meetings with managers. The managers would state their qualifications and experience to give the guests an idea of Nagarjuna's capabilities.

Raju would also invite them to dinner where the guests could get to know and interact with the team in a more informal setting. Important visitors would also be asked to plant saplings, and a small plaque with their names would be placed by the sapling. Raju insisted that all his factories had ample plants and greenery with ponds and trees. Each factory would also have a horticulture consultant to whom the clients would be introduced. Clearly, his exposure abroad was being combined with the best of eastern hospitality, and Rao was soaking it all in.

The Nagarjuna Group would grow to become a billion-dollar company, but back then, it was small. The early days at Nagarjuna Steel were great learning, according to Rao, for many reasons, the most obvious of them being that he was always spending time with the founder. 'I was always with Raju … so naturally, it was management, entrepreneurship, everything—starting from zero to move into some domain… He was a great networker, which was his strength. With him we met everyone—heads of banks, politicians, fellow industrialists.'

During those initial days at Nagarjuna Steel, Rao's own ambitions started to take shape.

'One of the advantages of proximity to people who are big achievers is that after some time, you start wondering that this guy does not seem any more intelligent than me, he does not speak as well as I do—what he can do, even I can do. And that realization is required, especially in our country, where entrepreneurship was essentially restricted to a few communities,' Rao says.

Given his experience at Union Carbide, at first, Rao's role was deemed to manage production and personnel. A critical recruitment to be conducted was that of Nagarjuna's marketing manager, but as providence would have it, the candidate to whom Nagarjuna made the offer backed out just a week before he was meant to join.

This was a critical role at the company, and in a meeting called to discuss this issue, Raju came up with the following proposition. 'What does a good marketing man need? Good communication skills, good analytical skills, good human relations skills, and finally, he should have fire in the belly. I have come to the conclusion that you have all four of these,' he said to Rao.

'Because of your industrial engineering and operations background, you have tremendous analytical skills. You have good speaking skills. As personnel manager, you have developed good people skills. And finally, because you have left a big multinational and would not want to fail here, you will have fire in your belly. So, you take the job.'

Even though Rao was a tad deterred by his lack of experience in marketing, he decided to accept the challenge while continuing to work with Raju. In due course, Rao would run one of its ventures called Nagarjuna Strapping Systems, which made steel belts for packaging.

Nagarjuna Steel made a strong start and achieved profits in its first year itself. Raju started looking for new projects to invest in. Given the closed Indian economy at that time, both imports and exports were significantly curtailed and foreign companies could only enter India through collaboration with local players. So he did the smart thing. He sent Rao and other senior colleagues to the USA to visit various plants and evaluate opportunities for manufacturing steel tubes and steel strapping (used typically for packaging industrial products).

While Signode was clearly one of the leading strapping and industrial packaging companies in the world, Rao had exercised his American experience in order to make the partnership come alive. He had travelled to Signode's headquarters in Glenview, Illinois, where he visited their manufacturing plants and offices. He sat out of the conference room where he worked and met with managers who updated him on their plants and products. Amongst the things that stood out in Rao's mind were the American predilection for valuing time as professionals: All his meetings went bang on time. The other was the high level of automation at the plants, which included nail-making, tool-making and seal-making, and even a robotized mail delivery system.

The trip was fruitful, and when Rao came back, he brought with him two prospective partnerships.

Sensing they could rope in an American partner with strong industrial and packaging technology, Rao decided to form an Indo-American partnership with Signode Packaging Systems (for steel strapping), and a technical alliance with Allied Tube and Conduit.

Rao joined Nagarjuna Signode as co-founder and managing director, with a 12 per cent ownership in the new company for Rs 30 lakh (Raju invested 28 per cent, Signode put in 36 per cent and the rest was to be raised through a public issue).

The inauguration of the Nagarjuna Signode company in India was not without its due share of state importance. The chief guest for the inauguration was none other than Chief Minister N.T. Rama Rao.

NTR, as he was referred to nationally, was a charismatic actor and film producer-turned-political leader and would be the chief minister of Andhra Pradesh for three terms over seven years. In a contrarian address, Signode executive Lee Flandreau would say that boosting revenue in strapping sales would be a slow process. Initially, he was right, and the company was not profitable. It was a difficult time for the company, and it was a challenge to hire and retain employees.

Nagarjuna Signode, however, did become profitable in the medium term. A few years later, Nagarjuna went ahead and sold its shares in Signode's IPO, thus making Signode the majority shareholder.

Signode's IPO was a success and was oversubscribed twice. Since it was a joint venture between an Indian company and an American company, the IPO was well received. Some of the company's strengths were that it had a modern plant, American management policies and training structure, and an MD who was educated and trained abroad—Nrupender Rao.

According to those who recall the development, the main objects of the venture were multi-focused. They included buying ferrous and non-ferrous metal-melting furnaces and rolling mills, and doing business as traders, manufacturers and fabricators of ferrous and non-ferrous ingots, blocks, billets, slabs, sheets, hot-rolled and cold-rolled steel strips, strips with edges, coated strips, steel strappings of various ranges of tensile strength, seals of various types, and non-metallic strapping systems.

Thus began Rao's first real experience of entrepreneurship with Nagarjuna Signode in 1981. Nagarjuna Signode gave Rao what he had never had before. Hands-on experience in setting up a company, operating, marketing and most importantly, dealing with foreign partners. No MBA course or college could have taught him to do any of that.

The one problem that Signode faced at that point was that Indian businesses were not very conscious of packaging and, therefore, ignorant about the company's products.

Rao explains, 'Until liberalization in the early to mid-1990s, everything was in very short supply, and so manufacturers did not really care about packaging—as long as they produced, there was demand. Companies were literally begging the government for licences to import steel and were running after local producers for supply. So packaging was always a low priority for manufacturers.'

What it meant was that he had to expend huge amounts of effort to sell Nagarjuna Signode's products and the company ended up with depleted funds. Entrepreneurship was not going to be easy, Rao was learning.

Right about the time Signode was going through its own twists and turns, Rao's second daughter, Avanti, was born in a Hyderabad nursing home. Rao was scheduled to fly to Chicago for meetings with Signode and, unable to cancel at short notice, made his wife promises to make it up to her. Signode products also had tremendous applicability in wagon loading, and Rao and his team travelled to Kolkata, where they met with general managers of steel plants as well as railway officials. After multiple rounds of discussion, they agreed to use the Signode style of wagon loading on a trial basis from Bokaro to Bombay.

Having bagged an order, Rao flew from Hyderabad to Kolkata and then went by car to Bokaro and Ranchi. He went by car all night, and then, as his luck would have it, the car stalled in the morning. So, he went to the local automobile repair shop. 'It will take several hours to repair,' Rao was told. He thought for a few minutes and then looked at the mechanic's motorcycle. Ten minutes later, Rao was on the bike and headed to Bokaro, where he made his appointment with the MD on time. The Signode machines were competitive with the Japanese ones they were using, and as things progressed, they got the order.

In conversation with Raju about the deadlock, he was given the suggestion that Rao approach the International Finance Corporation (IFC), Washington DC. It was a good idea, but Rao was hesitant due to Nagarjuna Signode's modest business. Raju said, 'So what if you are small; there is nothing wrong in that. Just go ahead and try. Tell them that we are doing some great things and see if they want to join us.'

Rao took the advice and acted upon it. IFC gave the Nagarjuna representatives a warm reception in the USA. While they were indeed sceptical about the size of the projects, they were excited at the thought of supporting the technocrat entrepreneurs and finally agreed to take equity in all three Nagarjuna group companies. Of course, Nagarjuna and Rao needed capital to finance the Signode, Tubes and Steel projects, so they visited IFC to apply for debt finance. While Signode was a joint venture partner, IFC insisted on a steel guarantee loan to fund any projects. That meant Rao and the team visited Washington many times before IFC finally approved their proposal.

Signode took over the JV, and the guarantees came from Nagarjuna Steel.

An unforeseen part of the Signode journey led Rao to make a passing acquaintance with an industrial tycoon who was also dreaming big. He visited Bombay post the approval of the Signode proposal, and at that juncture, thanks to ICICI, he had a meeting with Dhirubhai Ambani, the founder of Reliance Industries, with whom he had a brief tête-à-tête at an IFC congress. At the time, Rao was generating a revenue of around Rs 10 crore and Ambani was at approximately Rs 100 crore. He smiled and told Ambani that he would catch up in three or four years and be at Rs 100 crore, too. Ambani, equally game for sporting banter, responded, 'My friend, when you reach Rs 100 crore, I will have reached Rs 1,000 crore,' with a big smile that resulted in collective laughter.

That experience with IFC taught Rao to never underestimate one's opportunities. However, low demand was still an issue. Rao spent most of his time travelling, either within the country to market his products or to the USA, to manage the foreign partners. He had to focus on selling the entire concept, the benefits of spending additional amounts on packaging, on account of savings through lesser spoilage during transportation.

He would make elaborate presentations using financial models and studies to demonstrate his point. It was time-consuming and frustrating work, but Rao powered on and persisted. 'When an entrepreneur makes a loss, he goes through problems. But once you are in, you are in,' he later said.

The business made a loss in the first year, and some amount of refinancing was required again in the second year. Nagarjuna Signode rode through the storm and ultimately emerged as a blue-chip company. The lesson: When selling a superior, niche product, patience is the key.

In the meantime, Raju, who was clearly exhibiting signs of being a serial entrepreneur, had already embarked on a new venture—Nagarjuna Fertilizers. That meant Nagarjuna Steel had a leadership void, so he roped in Rao to help out with that, in addition to Nagarjuna Signode. Since the fertilizers division needed more capital, Raju also decided to sell his stake in Nagarjuna Signode.

Raju's stake was bought by an investor (a stockbroking firm) from Kolkata, who intended to play out till the stocks would be bought back by Signode and could be sold in the open market, Rao would later learn. The other side-effect that manifested was that after Raju's exit, the US partner began to exert more influence on company's operations. That was not something Rao felt comfortable with, but with the share price going up, Rao decided to sell his stake as well.

It was not an easy call. 'When you start a company, the relationship is almost like a mother and baby; you really get attached entirely—not only physically and mentally, but also emotionally.' Financially, however, the sale came as a windfall since Rao's 3,00,000 shares were worth almost Rs 15 crore, a huge amount of money forty years ago.

Meanwhile, there were other significant changes afoot. Raju's son was taking over the reins of Nagarjuna Steel, and Rao decided to transition onwards. Raju asked him to stay on, but Rao knew that in an organization, there had to be a single head calling the show. He had also learnt the most valuable lesson for an entrepreneur, which was that unless you work for yourself, for your own corporation, you would always be answerable to a boss and subject to changes you would never have any control over.

Signode was finally taken over by Illinois Tool Works, but Rao had a brand-new world waiting for him to explore. It was in the form of a company called Pennar that was alive, had licences and was legitimate but non-performing. His next move could not have been planned any better.

Hyderabad Management Association presents Nrupender Rao (seated) the Lifetime Achievement Award in 2017 at KLN Prasad Auditorium in Hyderabad.

Rao receiving the Distinguished Alumnus Award and Gold Medal from Prime Minister Manmohan Singh, at Indian Institute of Technology Kharagpur, 2011.

Receiving the Highest Tax Payer Award from the IT Department, Andhra Pradesh in 1995.

Rao at around age two at his father's residence, Domalguda.

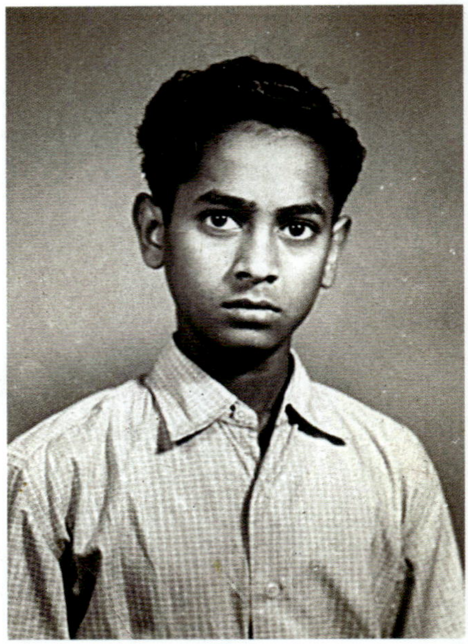

Rao at age twelve posing for a family photo at home.

Nrupender Rao and Rajyalakshmi at their wedding reception held at Exhibition Grounds, Hyderabad.

The Rao family at son Aditya's wedding reception at the Novotel Hotel Hyderabad, 2010. L to R: granddaughter Saanvi, son-in-law Sridhar Chelikani, Nrupender Rao, wife Rajyalakshmi, son Aditya, daughter-in-law Sudeepta, daughter Arathi, daughter Avanti, grandson Ribhu, son-in-law Subbarao Govardhanagiri, grandson Advitheey.

Graduation day: At Purdue University, Lafayette, Indiana, 1967.

At home in Jubilee Hills with the family. Clockwise from bottom left: Nrupender Rao, granddaughter Rithvi, daughter-in-law Sudeepta, son Aditya, wife Rajyalakshmi and grandson Reyansh.

At the ancestral family home in Domalguda. Standing L to R: brother-in-law M.V. Rajeshwar Rao, Nrupender, sister Rupa, sister Renuka, brother Naresh, brother-in-law Dr Muralidhar Rao. Sitting L to R: sister Ratnamala, father J.V. Narsing Rao, nephew Ajay, mother Radha Devi, nephew Srinath, sister Rekha.

Friends always lunch together: Monthly get-togethers with childhood, school and university friends from Little Flower High School and Nizam College. Standing behind Rao from L to R: Sheshadri, Prabhakar, Ram Mohan, Rangareddy, Narasimha Reddy, K. Gopal, Dr Prithvipathi, Wing Commander Bhushan, Mrs Laxmi (wife of Dr Prithvipathi), Bizzul Ashok, Hanumanth Reddy.

Gang of three. R to L: Ashok Srivastav, Rao and Devendra Mishra, former students from Indian Institute of Technology Kharagpur relive the good times.

Nrupender Rao displays a copy of his NASA scientist friend Suresh Kulkarni's book called *Rocket Man*.

Rao organizes a get-together for friendly visitors Rajiv and Preeti Tandon, at an Indian Institute of Technology reunion, at Alankrita Resort in Hyderabad, circa 2008.

Nrupender Rao in front of the Swami Vivekananda statue he helped build, in Tank Bund Hyderabad, during the celebrations held on his birthday.

In Hyderabad, making a gift of the Bhagavad Gita recordings to Swami Ranganathananda, one of the senior-most spiritual leaders within the Ramakrishna order.

Visiting a street named after Swami Vivekananda in Chicago, near the Art Institute, where the leader delivered his iconic speech, circa 2012.

Nrupender Rao shares his learnings with students at Dhruva College, Hyderabad, circa 2012.

Breaking new ground: With friend and mentor K.V.K. Raju (L), Founder of Nagarjuna Group of Companies at the inauguration of Pennar's aluminium factory in Nagpur, Maharashtra.

Sharing notes: Rao with Manish Sabharwal (R) who worked in his office and later went on to found Teamlease.

Managing the ground realities: Rao at the construction of the Pennar Aluminium factory in the early nineties.

Felicitating team spirit at the Annual Family Day celebration at Pennar's factory site.

With marketing guru Philip Kotler, the father of modern marketing, at an event in 2014, in Hyderabad.

Introducing N.T. Rama Rao, Chief Minister of Andhra Pradesh, at a corporate function, circa 1984.

Swapping insights: Rao in a lighter moment with Indian diplomat and economist Dr Abid Hussain at a business get-together.

Rao in conversation with present-day vice president of India, Venkaiah Naidu, on business and the state of the nation.

At the big table: Talking business with Prime Minister Rajiv Gandhi, in the late 1980s.

Meet and greet: Welcoming First Lady Hillary Clinton at an Indo-American Chamber of Commerce meet.

An unusual hitch-hiker: Rao's photograph of a bear approaching a car during one of his trips to Yellowstone, USA, in 1967.

Big wheels keep on turning: Pennar Industries factory at Patancheru for cold-rolled steel.

Custom-designed metal building systems at a Pennar Factory in the USA.

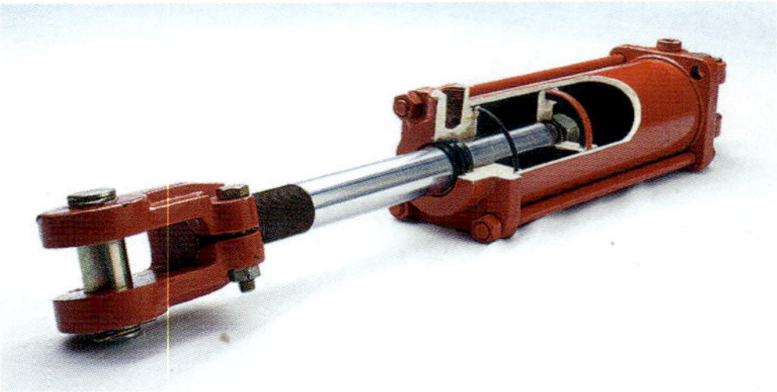

A hydraulics system used in tractors, off-highway vehicles and other machines made at Pennar's Chennai plant.

Machines at play: Industrial robots at work at Pennar's Chennai plant.

Pennar's solar module photovoltaic facility at Sadashivpet, Hyderabad.

Desalination plant built by Pennar.

# 6

# A Steel River and the Banyan Tree Business Model

POPULAR WISDOM SUGGESTS THAT A COMPANY CAN BE best understood by examining who its lawyers, auditors and bankers are. And the fastest way to get to know a person is either to travel with them or to look at the books they are reading and what their library looks like.

Inside Nrupender Rao's home, adjoining his primary living room on the ground floor, is his home office. It features two working desks with arm-chairs as well as a seating area for guests. And lining the walls, in glass-fronted shelves and cupboards, are at least a thousand books.

There are scores of publications on the philosophy of Sri Ramakrishna, the mystic saint who started a doctrine of life which was inherited by his protégé, Swami Vivekananda. There are also multiple biographies on both spiritual leaders, as well as many of the books they had written and those written by their followers.

Of course, not all the books here are religious texts. There are shelves with several large publications on yoga, on the history of India, and the history of Hyderabad. Another shelf, organized thematically, holds paperbacks on business and management. This shelf includes the surprising addition of modern titles such as *Drive* by Daniel Pink, works on Indian family businesses, on the transformation of India, on the shortage of water and how it would impact society, as well as books by management gurus Ram Charan and Richard Thaler. There is one shelf devoted to books about relieving tension, depression and anxiety. There were also biographies and other works by J.R.D. Tata, Sam Pitroda, Verghese Kurian, Thomas Harris and Malcolm Gladwell.

Another shelf features a set of books by Khushwant Singh, which perhaps achieves the same objective.

There is plenty of lighter fare as well but these belong to Rao's wife: Christie and Grisham authored mystery novels and legal thrillers filled with characters who were larger than life, with their novels constructed around plot lines that addressed a diverse range of subjects from social justice to whodunnits.

Unlike in the homes of most industrial houses, there are no expensive works of art or personal photographs with the rich and famous to be found anywhere in this library. Instead, the images adorning the walls are of Swami Vivekananda and one or two of the owners of the house. The furniture is sturdy mahogany, and the vibe is more college library than corporate office.

Overall, the room tells any visitor that its primary inhabitant is an individual with a sense for structure and possessed of deep interests that have been followed consistently over the years. This is also the room where Rao conducts several meetings with his business partners, senior employees, foreign guests, and local political leaders.

---

Rivers in India are not just water bodies that flow into the sea. Rivers are intrinsically woven into the very fabric of being and embody how closely man is related to nature. Rivers are seen as mother figures, nourishing and sustaining all those around, and even calming turbulent minds. Equally, rivers are seen as unpredictable, capable of turning malevolent and destroying the very ecosystem that it has nourished and supported. Literary works dwell upon the various facets of rivers and often speak of the arduous struggle men face when trying to triumph over nature in the form of rivers.

India is home to some eight or nine larger rivers, including the Ganges, the Jhelum, the Chenab, Yamuna, Kaveri and Godavari. There are also hundreds of other smaller watercourses that criss-cross the landscape of the subcontinent across states north, east, west and south. It is one such river that inspired Nrupender Rao, and he named his company after it.

The Pennar, also known as the Penneru, Penna, Pinakini, or Pennai, flows through Karnataka and Andhra Pradesh. It is not a large river, flowing just 600 kilometres before it merges with the Bay of Bengal. But it is a river that has inspired umpteen Telugu poets and authors. Rao never had a choice in the name of the firm he bought since it was a pre-existing steel company licence which had no assets. The name of the company was Pennar Steels, and he did not change the name. There was not a compelling reason to do so, but he was of the view that a company—like a river—should flow naturally, and so he let it remain.

Pennar, a company that started in 1975, had more than its name in common with the river it was named after. That is, in a small, almost insignificant way. The company had been started by two traders from Andhra Pradesh, who set up a cold rolling steel unit in Nellore. They had bought the land needed for the plant and had procured the appropriate licence. But, for various reasons, the unit did not take off, and the Andhra Pradesh Industrial Development Corporation (APIDC) told Nrupender Rao that he could buy it if he wanted.

The land that the traders had acquired was adjoining Signode land. Rao took this as a sign. It was almost as if providence was whispering in his ear. So, seeing an opportunity to be his own boss, to create a brand-new company and to take a stab at being an employer, Rao decided to buy up Pennar Steels. It was not cheap at Rs 18 crore back then, but Rao had the tacit support of Raju who supported and encouraged him to grow a business, even if it would end up being a competitor. Rao put in his own funds, got APIDC funding, and raised the rest through an issue of public equity.

Even as he went through the various steps of raising the money needed, Rao's mind went back to his days in the USA and the conversations he had with his room-mate about India's population advantage. 'So many people, so many lives, but not enough jobs,' he remembers saying back then. Now, with his own company, if he could create employment for a few thousand lives, he would be doing his bit in the dissipation of economic freedom and independence, the kind of which was never possible before.

While setting up as an entrepreneur was a huge step for Rao, practically all it meant was taking a few steps away from Nagarjuna Signode's factory at Isnapur, Hyderabad; Pennar was literally next door.

Back in the seventies and eighties, setting up shop independently was risky. Capital was not available for brand-new ventures. Other than the very large corporations that included the Tatas, Birlas and other family-run conglomerates, the consequence of failing at a new business could be nothing short of catastrophic. This was also a time when there was no private equity industry in the country, no venture capital, and local investment banks that included the three Ks were just about getting started. The Kothari–Kampani–Kotak trio dominated corporate finance—Hemendra Kothari, Nimesh Kampani and Uday Kotak headed the successful Indian financial powerhouses, DSP Merrill Lynch, JM Morgan Stanley and Kotak Mahindra Finance.

For Rao, the choices were fairly limited. He could not take the reins of running a family business because, given his father's career, there *was* no business to turn to. He could have joined another large industrial business house like Larsen & Toubro (L&T) or the Tatas or the Birlas, but it was clear to him that such careers and professional adventures would not be very different from what he had already experienced over the last few years. Besides, he was increasingly of the opinion that if he were to become the technocrat that he had been educated and trained for, he would have to start out on his own.

His family was settled and in place, with his wife overseeing the household and raising the children and offering him the moral and emotional support he needed. His return to India was complete in terms of both cultural and professional orientation. Rao was ready to run a company of his own, and he took the plunge.

Rao's industrial journey with Pennar started in 1987, with the setting up of a cold-rolled steel complex on a site at Isnapur near Hyderabad with a capacity of thirty thousand tons per annum. The site was designed by industrial and plant engineering consultants Mecon and constructed by Asia Engineering Company. Pennar Steels was a modern factory with a Z-Mill or Sendzimir Mill, which was a machine for rolling steel. Unlike other traditional rolling mills, this twenty-high cluster mill configuration used cascaded supporting rolls to apply force on the small work rolls in the centre.

What that did was allow the application of a higher roll pressure without bending work rolls; bending could cause poor metal quality. The net result was that very hard and elastic materials could be rolled in it.

Apart from that, Rao saw that annealing furnaces, a nitrogen plant and a conveyor were installed at the plant. Annealing is a heat treatment process used typically in steels to reduce hardness, increase ductility and help eliminate internal stresses.

The designers also set up an office block and a conference room. Rao made sure of other lighter touches as well. A mango orchard, rows of palm trees and mannequins of penguins and ducks at intersections on the driveways added a dash of humour and brought a smile to the faces of visitors.

With all that laid in place, business—thanks to Rao's earlier experiences—took off with aplomb.

In the very first year of operations, Pennar achieved cash profits and followed them up with profits and dividends in the second year. Buoyed by continuous growth in turnover and profitability year-on-year, Pennar expanded its capacity to fifty thousand metric tons per year.

All that time, playing in the background of Rao's mind, was Raju's operating model: Take an entrepreneurial employee or manager and get him to put his skin in the game, put him in charge of the existing company and move on to establishing another business. It was a subconscious management style that was to play out for Rao in his own turn as his company grew.

Meanwhile, Pennar started to make speciality value-added steels and value-added engineering components. Almost every bumper in a Tata truck at a certain point in time was made by Pennar. Seeing that the model of steel was better maximized for growth and expansion when bundled with parallel industries that included oil and gas, and other hard-hat sectors, Rao began to take stock of how to move to the next level of growth and lined up the chess pieces on his board. Even while he was doing that he would not forget from time to time to visit the birthplace of his father. In the decades to follow, Rao would even build a statue there in his memory as a token of gratitude for all the values, knowledge and wisdom he had received from him.

---

One of Rao's colleagues at Pennar who would serve as a key executive and prove to be a top managerial resource for Rao was Ananth Reddy. Reddy had begun his corporate life as a quality manager at the industrial and aeronautics giant HAL (Hindustan Aeronautics Limited) before he started at Nagarjuna in the early seventies.

Reddy, who would officiate as president of the group in the years to come, was a hands-on manager who kept long hours and ran a tight ship. 'Rao's marketing and communications were nothing short of excellent for an industry that was largely technical and stuffy in nature,' Reddy observed. When he exited Nagarjuna and took the call to start afresh, there were very few hiccups.

Even as Rao was setting up the foundation of his new group, India and the national business scene itself was undergoing changes silently but swiftly. Before the country saw economic liberalization roll out in the nineties, it was said that large corporations never had clients but had captive hostages because customers were so starved for choices when it came to vendors, suppliers and commercial partners. Indeed, the very manner in which business was seen and run by large corporations was different. Big companies did not have human resources divisions; they had 'admin' offices. They never had what is today referred to as a finance division; instead, they had accounting departments. An IPO itself was more like venture capital for companies than an exit for private equity investors.

For Rao, the existing template and benchmark, whether he consciously followed it or not, was that of Raju's Nagarjuna when it came to business and corporation building. Nagarjuna, which began as Nagarjuna Steel and then diversified into multiple parallel industries that included oil and gas, chemical and fertilizers, was a prime example of a successful child of the Licence Raj era.

The Licence Raj was a reference to regulations driven by bureaucrats. These regulations and rules were required to set up and run any Indian business between 1951 and 1991. In hindsight, the government had resorted to that sort of a system so that it could effectively exercise a modicum of control over industries under the Industries (Development and Regulation) Act, 1951.

Licences were issued, and along with them came particulars that included what could be made, where it was to be made, how much could be made and even when those volumes could be increased. Raju based his growth model for Nagarjuna on those conditions and used ventures like Nagarjuna Fertilizers to scale up the group. For Rao, as it would have been for any manufacturing entrepreneur in his shoes, the template was clear and obvious: Adopt the Banyan Tree Model.

The banyan tree, native to India and other parts of the subcontinent, is a large tree (a species of the fig tree) which is known for its aerial prop roots. That is, roots come down from the branches and, over time, begin to resemble a tree trunk. In effect, a banyan tree is supported by these umpteen root-branches and does not fall even in the most severe storm. It is like a business. Any business requires a foundation to grow, but like a banyan tree, that growth needs to come with constant improvement of strength.

At any rate, in the immediate moment, Pennar seemed to have potential to grow.

R. Rajamani, who was managing director of Pennar Steels and later also ran Pennar Refineries, was with the group for over a decade. 'I saw an ad for a job with them in the papers and applied, and that is how I landed up with them,' remembers the executive who lives in Chennai now. Rajamani was an engineer by training. He had specialized in metallurgy and had worked for a variety of large companies across India and had set up factories and the like.

Today, looking back, he says there are extremely few like Rao who would not only enable but also empower managers to make decisions based on their own instincts, 'You had absolute freedom to execute your objectives,' he recalls. 'We made profit from year one at Pennar Steels and were doubling virtually every year for the next few.' For a new player, the company was very profitable. Rao saw the growth as indication that it was time to create more companies which in turn would create what he wanted most: more jobs.

Rajamani emphasized that 'his basic idea was to provide employment to people, not to generate windfall profits or grow market cap to massive proportions.'

With Rajamani on board to run Pennar Steels, Rao now had the flexibility to turn his attention to other ventures. Equally important, it freed him up to dive deep into the world of corporate networking, something that called upon him to meet various people, shake many hands and plug into professional associations.

By 1987, once he had started running his own company, Rao began to tune into the kind of corporate networking and business involvement that is vital to the existence of large corporations. He started the Indo-American Chamber of Commerce's (IACC) division for Andhra Pradesh, and because Signode had the right percentage of American ownership (20 per cent), he was eligible for chairmanship. He started as vice-chairman and, a year later, assumed the office of chairman of the IACC. In that role, Rao would go on to fraternize with some of the country's established as well as emerging corporate brass that included Kotak Mahindra Bank's Uday Kotak, Raymond's Vijaypath Singhania and Ranbaxy's Bhai Mohan Singh, amongst others.

As chairman of IACC, Rao put his marketing skills to work, setting up the body's annual session as an event to remember and which members recall as having a traditional 'chowki-dinner' served on individual personalized, low four-sided tables at the Qutub Shahi tombs with Pakistani ghazal singer Mehdi Hasan performing for them. Always well-known, Rao was starting to become a high-profile figure in his own low-profile manner. His growth was not going unnoticed.

In 1989, N.T. Rama Rao, who was then chief minister of Andhra Pradesh, called Rao for a sit-down at his office. The minister exchanged pleasantries and then swiftly got down to business. 'I am looking for medhaavis (wise men) to assume the chairmanships of important state corporations,' said the chief minister. Rao assumed he was being asked for suggestions, and promised to keep his eyes and ears open. He told NTR that he would get back with some suggestions soon. Before he could do that, NTR's personal assistant and chief of staff called Rao. The CM had made an appointment, he told Rao. He had decided upon the new chairman of the Andhra Pradesh Industrial Infrastructure Corporation (APIIC)—Nrupender Rao.

Rao took a deep breath, and another. It was an honour, sure, but he wanted to steer clear of politics. He made a mental note to visit the Ramakrishna Math early the next day.

The Math was a ten-acre spiritual oasis opposite the Indira Park in Domalguda in the middle of the bustling metropolitan city that was Hyderabad. With well-designed shrine-like structures amidst large, neatly manicured gardens and an overarching air of tranquillity and learning, it was a place Rao had begun to visit regularly. His early attraction to the

Ramakrishna Mission and Swami Vivekananda's teachings had only grown stronger over time.

At the Math, Rao headed to the inner sanctum to meet Swami Ranganathananda who was president there. He spoke to the Swami about his concerns regarding getting involved with politics when all he wanted to do was set up businesses that would employ people. The holy man heard him out, and finally asked just one question: 'Did you solicit the position?' The answer was a flat—and very firm—'no'. Swami Ranganathananda, equally firmly, told Rao: 'Then accept it.' And so Rao did take the post.

As chairman of APIIC, he got to rub shoulders with those in public office, politicians and IAS officers. He went on to preside over the body for a year and regularly attended meetings at Gandipet, which he would describe as long, sometimes arduous, but always rewarding in their provision of insight and know-how on how business societies and communities were working. He continued being the management student attending lectures and events by the likes of C.K. Prahlad and other business gurus in his quest for expanding his mind.

---

Back at business, Rao never stopped learning from Nagarjuna. As a company, Nagarjuna blossomed, thanks to its steels and fertilizer businesses. But it also had a financial services venture that it had incorporated in 1982, and whose business was to provide lease finance, hire purchase, investment finance and management services.

Seeing the inclusion of such a business as strategic and useful for a business house that was involved in manufacturing and industrial services, Rao took a page out of Raju's book and replicated the model once again.

He chalked up a finance company called Pennar Finance and opened it for business in 1991.

At Pennar, Rao was known for his penchant for bright young executives. He could spot talent easily and would give these young people a chance to run the business. As part of his nurturing of talent, Rao also took the effort to choose the ones with the most potential to work in his office for short periods of time, either as his chief of staff or as executive assistants. The idea behind this was to create a set of people who could effectively relay and execute his decision-making and maintain the ethos that Rao wanted in his offices. In turn, these young people would share insights and provide their worldviews on business.

A friend of Rao's, a police officer, asked him in passing if Rao would consider his son as an executive assistant for a short period. Rao agreed, and asked the boy, Manish Sabharwal, to come to the office for a conversation and interview. He found Sabharwal to be a curious whippersnapper and hired him.

Sabharwal says Rao enjoyed shooting the breeze with him, and also had intellectual debates on business. He recalls that as a boss, one of Rao's favourite words was 'drama'. 'Watch the drama going on,' Rao would tell him or 'same usual drama' or 'back to drama'. The other word that Rao used a lot, especially when speaking about entrepreneurship, was maya.

Maya, in Hindu philosophy, is the principal concept which manifests, perpetuates and governs the illusion and dream of duality in the universe. For some mystics, this manifestation is real, but it is a fleeting reality; it is a mistake, although a natural one, to believe that maya represents a fundamental reality or truth.

Maya, according to Rao, was the reference point he would bring up when asked by Sabharwal why certain things were working out in the manner that they did in business.

Sabharwal would often thrust and counter his mentor, suggesting that he ought to run more diligence in the manner in which he was planning his new ventures and business projects. Invariably, the answer was that in business and in entrepreneurship, it was impossible for the CEO to have all the answers before he embarked on a journey. If indeed he did have all the answers, then it was management he was affecting, not true entrepreneurship, which, by definition, involved some amount of fumbling in the dark and taking chances.

These congenial debates and discourses would go on. The younger man would insist that different models were needed and the CEO would explain how existing models, with the notion of the company as a group or conglomerate, had worked with success in countries like Japan. Rao spoke of Japan's Zaibatsus or Korea's Chaebols. And this worked in India too, Rao would explain, pointing to the Nagarjuna group of companies. In due course, Sabharwal left to go get a business degree from Wharton, where he had gotten admission to pursue his master's in business. He committed to Rao that he would return to Pennar after he finished his schooling.

In the meantime, Rao was itching to set up more companies. Across the ecosystem, he was watched as larger groups including the Mahindras, the Birlas, and the Tatas, widened their footprint through a combination of large core industrial ventures that included backbone businesses and other sectoral ventures that either fit into their supply chain or then branched out into consumer-facing companies.

The way Rao saw it, Pennar was profitable, and the money was rolling in, but that was not his core objective. He wanted to drive employment; he wanted to be the largest employer in Andhra Pradesh—and even in the country. He would tell his colleagues and stakeholders, 'Money is fine, but with ideas, energy and people that rally around a cause, one could achieve anything on the planet.'

Things came to a head one morning in his office when Rao met two old friends—one, a former colleague.

That morning, like most days, Rao woke up at 4.30 to meditate. Never one for rote repetition of prayer and verse, he did believe in the concept of rebooting his mind and cleansing it of the clutter of unnecessary thought. By around 5.30 a.m., his colleague Vijay Puljal came by, and the two drove down to a nearby park to attend an hour-long open-air yoga session conducted by a teacher for a small group.

After yoga, Rao and Puljal walked around the park for a while, getting up to speed with the day's activities and going over the previous day's highlights. He got home before 8 a.m.

and read a few pages from the scriptures. He usually read some pages from the Bhagavad Gita, the Bible, the Koran, or the teachings of Zarathustra and Guru Nanak. In Rao's worldview, all religions preach the same, and the essence of religion is to be good. His plan was to eventually have read all the scriptures. He then had a light breakfast and left for the office at 9 a.m.

Rao's cabin was situated at Pennar's corporate office near Begumpet, Hyderabad. An office says plenty about its occupant, and his was all about being spartan; a utilitarian desk facing a handful of simple chairs, a stacked bookshelf in one corner, a computer, and a plant in another corner. The only splash of colour was a bright image on his desk. That was a smiling Swami Vivekananda. Also prominently displayed was a Vivekananda quote that read, 'Strength is life, weakness is death.'

After checking his schedule with Sunil Kuram, his assistant, clearing some routine jobs, and signing cheques, Rao got ready for his day's work. By 11 a.m., he was done with checking on things and chatting with other managers. That is when Rao asked Kuram to hold all calls except emergencies and settled down to talk business with a former colleague from Nagarjuna, P. Bhaskara Rao and Vijay Mishra.

Over coffee, the three agreed that they could not be getting into the realm of ventures that they knew nothing about. They thought they should stick to doing what they knew and understood best—engineering services or mainstream manufacturing. At that point, Rao exclaimed that they clearly could not get into setting up pizza chains or hotels. Any future business would have to be involved with metals in some way. The germ of the idea of Pennar Aluminium was born.

Aluminium, apart from being a highly consumed material across industries, was also a metal that was picking up in India, especially with the opening up of its markets post-liberalization. From buildings to trucks, trains, ships, planes, bikes, cars, and soft drink and food cans, aluminium was in demand. The metal had heat conductivity, durability, a high strength-to-weight ratio, and was low maintenance. It was used in electrical transmissions and distribution cables and power systems and substations.

In principle, the idea was not without merit because then, there were not very many players of substance in aluminium. Top companies included mostly state-run players such as Bharat Aluminium (owned by the Government of India), Balco, Nalco, and Indian Aluminium (owned by the Alcan group), the Aditya Birla-owned Hindalco and Malco.

Rao's plan to jump into aluminium was an extension of his overarching vision to grow Pennar beyond steel, look to increase its wingspan and become a player of significant scale and national impact. It would also mean that he would be able to ramp up on employment and the creation of livelihoods, the raison d'être for his entire business life.

At that time, setting up an aluminium plant in India required courage. Beyond the fact that the established players were already well-entrenched and possessed of large balance sheets, strong customer relationships and deep industry know-how, there was another primary hurdle or pain point for new players who wanted to get into the growing sector—licences.

As expected, for a business venture of scale in that era, the core challenge was to obtain a licence for manufacturing aluminium. The primary problem was getting a licence for manufacturing, but that was not something that daunted Rao at that point in time.

# 7

# A New Economy Also Means Hurdles, Setbacks and Meltdowns

'WHAT DO YOU THINK THE MAIN PURPOSE OF LIFE—anyone's life—is?' The question from a man of the cloth came with neither trickery nor condescension. It was also devoid of humour or sarcasm. There was no easy answer to deliver, given the environment that I found myself in. During one of my trips to Hyderabad, I drove down to the Ramakrishna Math in the city.

The centre, one of the two of its kind in the country, was an oasis of calm in a bustling metropolis bloated with infrastructural cholesterol and intellectual strife, as is the case with most large metropolises in the subcontinent. The campus included a temple, a library, a museum, and a bookstore, all set amidst neat gardens and greenery. There was a sense of all-pervading tranquillity. As it was originally conceived, the centre featured a Universal Temple named so that all people, regardless of religion, caste, gender and nationality could attend, and take part in prayer, meditation or worship.

I had entered the facility with a dual objective. For one, I was curious to see what lay behind the doors of what had been acclaimed by millions to be a seat of modern learning, spirituality and intellectualism. And two, I was simply curious to see what it was that had drawn Rao, a modern-day capitalist and technocrat, to not just visit here as much as he had done but also become as deeply involved with it in the manner that he had. A couple of kilometres away, at the junction of a highway, before entering the centre, was a large, thirty-foot-tall bronze statue of Swami Vivekananda that had been built, funded and set up by Rao as a tribute to a man he admired and revered.

Inside the centre, I waited for a few moments before I was led to the equivalent of the sanctum sanctorum of the head priest or Swami Jnanadananda, the president of the Ramakrishna Math for the Hyderabad centre.

A slight, elderly man with dark skin and piercing obsidian eyes, the priest took me in. He repeated the question, as I searched for what might be an answer that was close to the truth: 'What do you think … the main purpose of life is?' he asked again.

And then, as I failed to give deeper answers to his first question, he explained where he was coming from. 'The purpose is to realize God and to realize that we are all children of God,' he said.

'That is where the link often gets missed, and every scripture says this as well that we are all and ought to be divine by nature. Can you not see this universe … that this universe has a way when the earth rotates—there is some form of control and order, and there is some sort of system to it? This is the Vedas. It is knowing that the snake that bites the man and the man who is getting bitten are both driven by the same life force.'

Swami Jnanadananda paused, smiled and then said: 'Maybe I am getting too philosophical for you. But let us talk further about what you have come for.'

From him, I learned that Rao was someone who seemed to be concerned about social development and was constantly striving to see how he could support or contribute to causes that furthered both education as well as the propagation of the principles of the Ramakrishna Math and its philosophies.

The caveat: Swami Jnanadananda had not met Nrupender Rao as many times or knew him as well as the priest before him. 'I had limited contact and knew him for a short period of time,' I was told.

On one occasion, he said, he had asked Rao a seemingly simple question: 'How much Mala Japa do you do?' Mala japa is a way in which beads on a rosary are used to keep count of the number of times a mantra or saying is recited. Apparently, Rao, in all his years of being a follower of the mission, had never been asked that. It seemed to trigger a wave of emotion in him and threw him off balance.

The general and early impression Rao gave to those at the mission was that he was deeply inspired by Swami Vivekananda. Neither Swami Jnanadananda nor the other monks at the centre ever saw Rao as a man of commerce. On the contrary, he was seen and perceived by them as a kinsman and more like someone who was in tune with spirituality. He was driven by the Ramakrishna Mission. In his effort to promote the objectives of the mission, Rao spent money, time and energy gifting books from the centre to scores of young people.

He was also constantly striving to see if he could get more and more content from the mission to be included in academic curriculums in local schools. Above all, it was his humility and lack of ego that never failed to surprise those at the mission.

A younger monk at the institute remembered how Rao would, from time to time, come in and prostrate himself as a mark of respect to the presidents at the mission. Most of the other monks in attendance could not believe that the same man employed thousands of people and ran several factories across the state.

---

Rao looked very serious. Then he laughed out loud. He was responding to a question that his childhood friend, Kulkarni, had thrown at him after he had received a full tour of his friend's home in Jubilee Hills. Kulkarni took in the patio, the home library, the study, the dining hall and finally the home gym, with its modern exercise equipment. 'Has it helped you at all?' he had asked.

The laugh had been preceded with a nod, a look of absolute seriousness and then a gesture to his own tummy. 'What do you think?' Those who knew him recall that despite being generally serious, Rao had a wry sense of humour. As he approached middle-age, he had become thicker-set and had a belly—and he was okay to laugh about it.

The truth was that running Pennar Steels and getting it off the ground left little time for Rao to exercise beyond what he did in the morning in terms of walks and light yoga. His new venture was also a distraction that he tinkered with and argued with himself and his team before he decided to take the plunge.

Once his mind had been made up on the call to dive into the aluminium business, Rao never held back. The toughest thing about getting into new industries then—obtaining permissions and licences—was actually a less formidable challenge for him. Coming from the background that he did, he approached the union minister for industry, who was aware of his professional experience and did not hesitate in issuing a manufacturing licence for Pennar. Once that was out of the way, Rao turned his attention to getting technical support for the new factory. Although it was still a metals factory, it demanded specialized know-how. Rao managed that by putting together a collaboration with a top French company called Pechiney, which had carved out a reputation for itself in the aluminium and packaging industry.

The plan was this: To roll out a state-of-the-art plant on a 220-acre plot in Nagpur, with an earmarked investment of around Rs 200 crore. Back then, it was a princely sum even for a large business house. Of course, Rao had the wherewithal to raise money and proceeded to rustle up the capital through an equity issue and debt from all-India financial institutions.

Why did he pick Maharashtra and not stick to Andhra Pradesh, specifically Hyderabad? Apparently, the decision to venture out of his neck of the woods was twofold and quite simple. Nagpur was selected because electricity was in abundant supply at that time, while most places in Andhra Pradesh had begun to see a shortage. The second and other advantage was that the plant was being set up during the regime of P.V. Narasimha Rao, who was not only well-acquainted with Rao but had, more importantly by then, ascended in his career to become Prime Minister of India.

While Rao always had conviction in his own abilities, that sort of connectivity in the business and political landscape gave him the confidence that if there were any bureaucratic red tape or obstacles to getting licences and permissions, he would be better placed in tackling and navigating around it.

Also, Rao had achieved what he wanted to in Hyderabad and his home state of Andhra Pradesh, businesswise, by the early nineties was rolling around, and the country had opened up with economic liberalization. The markets had welcomed unfettered competition. While any kind of big-ticket expansion brings with it risk and the possibility of failure, Rao took heart from the fact that by then, Pennar had shaped up into a full-service speciality steels company.

Pennar Steels or PSL started commercial production in 1988–89. It achieved full capacity utilization in the second year, made a profit, and declared dividends. The company had an annual production capacity of 36,000 tons. By 1995, the capacity was raised to 60,000 tons a year. There was a steady increase in production and sales from 1990 to 1996.

By 1997, revenue was up by more than double to Rs 320 crore from 1996, business was chugging along, it had reputable clients that included Tata Motors and L&T, and its growth extended to building out its steel as a brand as well.

Right about this time, Sabharwal had returned from the USA after completing his MBA at Wharton with a view to rejoining his former boss and mentor. Sabharwal was not entirely convinced about the viability of the aluminium project. He recalls that he did not see a detailed business case study and analysis of how the project was going to survive long term in the wake of intense competition, but there was only so much that he was going to argue with his boss.

Besides, he was well aware that business in India, regardless of liberalization, would still function with shades of the old-world Licence Raj. His mandate was to take Pennar Finance to the next level. The group had purchased a Chennai-based stockbroking firm called Paterson & Co., leading to the re-christening to Pennar Paterson Securities. The new company became the fifth-largest broking firm in Mumbai and the second-largest in Chennai, Sabharwal said.

If SBI or a banking consortium had lent Rs 50 crore, Pennar would kick in with a crore or two in funding. The whole system was geared for corporate houses, not individuals.

Inspiration for Pennar Paterson, at least in part, came from the experience of Nagarjuna's financial services branch which also ran its own NBFC. While the object of the Pennar NBFC was to finance companies that were setting up new factories and expansions with the last-mile or 'tail-end' financing, there were chinks in the business model that later surfaced.

Right before Pennar Aluminium was set up, Rao did what any emerging tycoon would have done. He hired top talent and engineers and a highly qualified CEO to chalk out the plans and land sites and then went and set up Pennar's plant and factory in Nagpur, Maharashtra, through a tie-up with Pechiney. The highlight included Prime Minister P.V. Narasimha Rao felicitating the opening of the plant.

Despite Pennar being much smaller than the existing aluminium players in India, Rao, ever the technocrat, had a clear goal. He wanted to set up a plant that was superior to its competitors. In that regard, Pennar Aluminium's rolling mill was the widest and the fastest in India and was more advanced than what even the Birlas had. For marketing, Rao tied up with Metallgesellschaft, a German company.

The plan had been executed, and Rao had completed phase one of what he wanted to do long term, which was to increase employment and grow Pennar into a business house with national interests. Due to aluminium being in short supply and partly due to the technological superiority of the plant, Pennar

Aluminium made a profit in its first year of operations in 1994. It had around 250 employees and was catering especially to the booming local automotive and real estate-related manufacturing sectors. Clients included Annapurna Foils and India Foils of Kolkata. Also, Maharashtra had long enjoyed a reputation for being a manufacturing hub, and the local area had several auto component makers with local offices and factories in the neighbourhood.

At around the same time, Rao was also pushing growth at Pennar into new directions by diversifying into different ventures.

The Pennar Group consisted mainly of PSL (the flagship), followed by Pennar Paterson Securities, Pennar Aluminium, Pennar Profiles, Pennar Chemicals, and Pennar Infotech. Pennar Infotech was started by Rao but mostly in the later years, taken over and run by his son-in-law Sridhar Chelikani. Pennar Chemicals was started before the aluminium plant and was making fuel and oil additives and had a tie-up with Elf of France (later merged with Total).

Rao also bought over an extrusion maker, Progressive Aluminum, for Rs 50 lakh and renamed it Pennar Profiles to expand the range of products offered by Pennar Aluminium. Aluminium extrusions are made by pushing billets into predesigned moulds under high pressure to create cross-sectional profiles. These are basically elongated pieces of aluminium custom-designed for a variety of different industrial uses.

Another venture happened more by chance, as happened quite commonly in those days. Rao was approached by the government of Tamil Nadu to set up a business in that state. The operation was an oil refinery. Given the shortage of oil and the difficulty in just getting basic government approvals for production, Rao saw this as having the potential to become a high-growth venture. So, he decided to partner with the Tamil Nadu government and relocate an existing refinery owned by Mobil.

Rao's advisors, as well as employees with Indian Oil, did warn him about the challenges in moving an entire refinery, but he saw the opportunity as a challenge. The Rs 600 crore project was backed by Mobil and the Tamil Nadu government, and Rao signed the deal.

---

Then, and earlier, Rao had forged relationships with investors from Kuwait.

Mr Al Sabah, a member of the Al Sabah family and also part of the ministry and the royal family, agreed to get on board as well because they strongly believed in the overall economic Indian growth story. The relationship had started when the conversation with Mobil (Canada) began. Advisers on the deal suggested talking to the Kuwaitis, as they felt there would be interest in those quarters for an oil business.

The first meeting took place at a conference hall at the Taj Mahal Hotel. Rao, Puljal and their associates waited in their suits and ties, expecting a formal engagement. Two Kuwaitis arrived—Mr Al Roumi and Mr Al Sabah. One was in traditional Arab garb and the other in jeans and a T-shirt. The one in the

Arab robes was the advisor, and the prince and minister he introduced was the young man in jeans. 'The presentation went very well, and the Kuwaitis committed to getting on board and, after having attended a few meetings in Hyderabad and Nagpur, became a partner,' said Puljal. The prince invested cash for an equity stake that translated to approximately 8 per cent, Puljal recalls.

And so, an advance was paid to Mobil for their refinery. Then 200 acres of land was purchased in Tamil Nadu, with intent to purchase another 800 acres in due course. Even as the oil business was being formulated, Pennar had gotten plenty on its plate.

---

Even while Rao and his managers were aiming to grow the business across different sectors, there was trouble brewing at Pennar's big bet in Maharashtra.

Harvard University management guru Michael Porter's theory of the five forces of market competition has been frequently studied in regard to industry analysis and especially in reference to the Indian aluminium trade. Porter's five principles include the threat of substitutes, bargaining power of customers, bargaining power of rivals, the threat of new entrants and finally, competitive rivalry.

While Rao was more than prepared for the first three, the last two in the form of Chinese exports became a spoiler that left little room for recovery. For a man used to taking risks that normally resulted in windfall gains, growth and success, the aluminium venture had started to seem like a misstep. At the point Pennar Aluminum was being planned, the customs duty for imports was around 450 per cent. But by the time the factory was up and running, duties had been rejigged and slashed by almost nine times to around 40 per cent in 1995. That meant that the homegrown advantage was facing decimation.

With the liberalization of the Indian economy making its effect felt towards the middle and later part of the 1990s, Pennar Aluminum started facing severe competition from foreign players, including companies from Korea. Bankers had already told Rao that it was going to be difficult to compete with the Birlas and the foreign competition, but no one had expected that it would happen as soon as it did. In a later magazine interview, reflecting back on those years, Rao said, 'When you are an entrepreneur, you do not listen to negatives; it is always positives. I thought that I would find my niche. An entrepreneur cannot always work with logic. If we had only cared to understand that (the impact liberalization would have on the Indian economy), we may have been more cautious.'

Indeed, Rao was not the only player in Hyderabad to have missed the gravity of the impact that liberalization had on their business. Deccan Cements also ran into trouble when they launched their finance arm, DCL Finance, which was started by a doctor who was an associate of some top executives at Deccan Cements. DCL Finance was primarily an auto finance company giving loans to customers to buy cars, but its lack of fiscal controls led the business to fail. Then there was GVK, which had a company called Novopan that made particle boards. That business also ran into trouble in part because of competition and being pushed over the edge by liberalization.

Despite all its windows of opportunity, aluminium also had its risks that included market and price fluctuations. While risks mostly remain in theory, sometimes the unthinkable happens, and they become a reality. For Pennar, it was a convergence of many of these issues. Its prices were unviable in the face of cheaper Chinese and American metals that were flooding the market. Another issue, says Sabharwal, was that 'across industries, older technology was facing competition, and at the same time, the Licence Raj ending meant corporate finance, steeped in old-world systems, was becoming unsustainable.'

'Most business leaders were only starting to understand the concept of asset-liability management, and it was not difficult for a business then to get caught between the winds of change into different economic regimes,' added Sabharwal. As the saying goes, it was a huge ask to expect corporate creatures bred in captivity to flourish in the wild.

Once the effects of liberalization started to play out, the heavy project cost also began to weigh the company down. Pennar Aluminium's balance sheet bloated, and as it would later become evident, the project's delays were not without their own cost.

The fact was that the aluminium project and business had been built and conceived around barriers to entering India, and if that linchpin was to come loose, then the company was on a very slippery slope. And sure enough, the linchpin came loose.

Rao waited for several years—seven, to be precise—for the tide to turn. But when he realized it was not going to and that aluminium had become a drag on the group's cash flows, he and his team embarked on a mission to fix the problem, with minimal job losses.

Attempts were made to keep Pennar Aluminium afloat by changing the business model from buying raw aluminium and selling converted material to purely doing conversion work on a contract basis.

None of that worked. Finally, it was declared a sick unit.

For someone whose key target was to maximize employment, the notion of having to lay people off was unfathomable. So, Rao met every major player, from Alcoa to Reynolds to Hindalco, in a bid to see if he could stem the bleeding and forge alliances or partnerships, but no one took the deal, says Sabharwal. The Birla-led Hindalco did show interest but pulled back only to show interest later when the company was seized by the Asset Reconstruction board and the lenders and put on the block.

Realizing he could not win, Rao took the hard call to hive off the aluminium operation despite the fact that it had drawn up almost Rs 200 crore in revenue in its first couple of years.

The Aditya Birla group finally acquired Pennar Aluminium from the Asset Reconstruction Company (Arcil) for Rs 185 crore in 2006; they bid Rs 10 crore more than the other bidders and said they would take the land, building and machinery.

Pennar offered Birla the company as well, but that was rejected, much to Rao's disappointment. Later, however, most of the employees were absorbed as part of the deal. Pennar officials say the bankers who were owed approximately Rs 200 crore were all paid off.

For Rao, this was perhaps his worst nightmare after his father's untimely death. He was distraught to see what could have been a game-changing venture crash and burn. In the end, Pennar Aluminium was reduced to being a shell company with no operations; it was being quoted at Rs 2.50 on the stock exchange.

His employees say that Rao took this on the chin. He never fired the top CEOs and managers in a bid to dodge responsibility and blame them for the failure. Indeed, that would have been the easy way out, to sacrifice some top executives and walk away blameless and unscathed. But that simply was not Rao's style from a spiritual or management standpoint.

Pennar Aluminium was Rao's first major failure. Sadly, it was not his last.

---

Pennar Finance (later renamed Pennar Paterson), the company Sabharwal was pushing, operated in a sector that was regulated—but which did not have the controls and checks as it has today. By 1999, the company was reporting severe cash flow problems due to a mismatch of assets and liabilities. In a painful turn of fortunes, the company was put under provisional liquidation by the Andhra Pradesh High Court.

Like many NBFCs then (and now IL&FS, whose NBFC-related meltdown led to a flurry of defaults across corporate India), it had issued a lot of loans but not received enough collateral in exchange.

Pennar Paterson had tried to monitor its lending habits by giving advances to companies that other blue-chip banks had also lent to. However, things came apart when borrowers such as Patheja Forgings and Kedia Distilleries could not repay what they had borrowed. Banks such as HDFC, ICICI and IDBI were first on the list to get paid, while smaller lenders took the bigger haircut, recalls Sunil Kuram, executive assistant to Rao. However, the issue was basically that the large banks had lent to these companies under secured debt arrangements (first charge on fixed and current assets) and that Pennar Paterson's investments were unsecured.

The banks were supposed to recover Rs 38 crore, including interest, that Pennar Paterson had been unable to recover from its borrowers, Puljal says. Pennar Paterson did have experts like the former chairman of the Bank of Baroda, S. Sivaramakrishna, advising them and on board as a vice president, but strategic mistakes were made. For one, Pennar focused on companies that suffered due to liberalization.

Of course, there were some local as well. There was a Maruti dealer in Hyderabad called Mahalaxmi Motors who took advances to buy and then sell 100 cars. After the loan was given, the company never repaid its dues. After getting the loan, the cars should have all been technically in the name of Pennar Paterson. Mahalaxmi Motors neither delivered the cars directly to Pennar nor did it return the money. 'That is how it started to go wrong,' remembers Puljal. Again, Pennar was not the only financial services company to stumble. 'The systems were simply not set up to protect financiers,' he adds. In fact, most companies that ventured into finance, and that included ITC Finance, DCL Finance, Lloyds Finance, Alpic Finance (from big pharma player Cipla) and also Nagarjuna Finance all bled and ran into the ground, he says.

During a meeting with Rao, Puljal remembers how his boss was fairly cool on the outside. 'The fact that he had loaned money to parties who went bust was out of his control and led him to turn his focus on one thing alone: getting back to steel and his core business.' On the inside, however, Rao was burning with disappointment. For the first time, he was receiving dozens of legal notices and facing litigation because checks issued by Paterson were not being cleared. Left with no choice, Pennar and Rao countersued their larger borrowers who had reneged on payment. The legal circus had become a merry-go-round of complaints and tussles within tussles that were dragging the business down. It was not what Rao ever wanted to get involved in. But, as he liked to say, if manufacturing was a bed of thorns, the financial world was riddled with pitfalls caused by regulations and laws, waiting to swallow the unwary.

Deep down, of course, he was upset that he had not undertaken the risk management necessary to evaluate whether unsecured lending was viable and which led larger, richer corporations to whisk away funds that belonged to smaller depositors within Pennar Paterson.

How much was due to smaller investors? Pennar officials say the amount was around Rs 10 crore and Pennar paid back close to 75 per cent of their total dues. That happened through a combination of personal cash, as well as plots of land that belonged to the promoters that were taken and then carved out into smaller plots and given to depositors. Puljal says that close to a hundred acres of land was given to depositors.

How did it all spiral out of control? S.V. Ramachandra Rao says that one of the things about Rao was that 'he tends to believe people and tries to see the best in people, and trusts them until they prove otherwise.' That could be a management strength and a weakness depending on the situation at hand.

Puljal, who was one of his top executives, started to sink into a morale-destroying funk as he saw Pennar's ambitious plans turn into a morass from which recovery seemed impossible. 'I am feeling depressed,' he would tell Rao. The reply, invariably, was that he needed to hang in there and that highs and unbelievable lows were both transient parts of the same illusion of business. 'Maya' is all it is Rao would say, and that the only true and real objective was to create jobs and provide livelihood. In classic style, Rao would tell Puljal to snap out of it, often adding that snapping out of it was only a matter of mindset and self-belief. 'Use it' and get back to work was Rao's advice.

Another long-time executive at Pennar who declined to be named but had been by Rao's side through key inflection points recalls that even while the aluminium business floundered, not once did Rao show any signs of despair or worry. 'Even as he was approaching the depths of failure many times, not once did his character ever change,' he said. 'That would be tested in the future time and again as he would have to endure more failures after aluminium as well.'

Why were so many of the new ventures going off track? One view is that being academically focused, Rao may have relied too much on elite management talent to suss out business opportunities and market analytics. This was at a time when the flow of information was less readily available than it is today, but that could not be the only factor.

Ramachandra, who was key in trouble-shooting a lot of the groups' irritants as a result of the businesses that went awry, noted that at any given time, there was 'elite management talent surrounding the chairman and feeding him points of view. While they were knowledgeable for sure; they may not have had a clear view of what was going on the ground.'

That must have been especially true in a world just getting used to moving out of an era dominated by the Licence Raj.

Ramachandra also points to another issue, that of a subset of managers who were used to functioning in a certain style that may not have been in sync for a new venture. 'Normally, a person could take a train from Hyderabad or Secunderabad at 10 p.m. and be in Nagpur, where the Pennar Aluminium plant was, by 6 a.m. to 7 a.m. the next day,' he observed. 'Instead, the existing style for some top managers would be to take a train to Mumbai, stay there overnight at a hotel and then fly down to Nagpur.' That all added to costs and project overruns when one calculates that there were several execs travelling back and forth for a couple of years like that.

Was Rao simply naive about how to run a business? The answer is no. His problem, as those close to him saw, was the inability to say no to people—and the inability to fire people. His burning desire to provide employment and livelihood to large numbers of people became one of his major challenges. 'Nrupender Rao was the first person I called at four in the morning years ago when I panicked when my wife had a heart attack,' Ramachandra said. 'He was the kind of promoter-boss who would have no qualms visiting his employees' homes, having them over to his home, spending time with them after hours, all in a bid to get to understand them better.'

Chandrasekhar Sripada, former general manager and head of HR for Pennar in the late nineties, says that he created systems processes and set up compensation for senior employees at the group, amongst other functions. 'He (Rao) was not a micromanager and always kept this eye on the big picture, and was accessible in every real sense.'

He knew not just employees, but also their wives, and their children personally.

He would go to homes of workers, even at the lowest levels and not just go there but even invite them to corporate functions. He did things like approve educational loans and advances for higher studies without setting a payback time frame for workers. 'Look after the people always, was the philosophy,' Sripada recalls, adding that every morning he would go into the office and call for his direct reports that included Sripada. He would then pull out from his pocket an assortment of little pieces of paper or chits. Half of them would be on recruitment and how some CEO was functioning, and the other half would be on which people needed support and help. This was done on an almost daily basis regardless of regulatory commitments and other business objectives that every CEO handled. 'It was not a tactical to-do list but a good to-do list.'

Could Rao have run things differently? And would things have changed because of that? Rao is not sure but, in hindsight, accepts that he went a bit overboard with the aluminium project. However, for other ventures, the economic environment was to blame. And in retrospect, he could also have gone a little slower in his rate of expansion and diversification. It is no secret that even the most able of managers cannot focus on more than one or two large complex businesses in totality; Rao, in his exuberance and enthusiasm to not miss out on growth, had diluted his focus in that regard.

---

Rao's perseverance and ability to fix problems were no less than his desire to build new ventures. 'Pennar Aluminium was the first to resolve a problem voluntarily after the ARC was established by SBI. It was our approach, our handover and our reach out to them,' Ramachandra said. 'Liabilities and litigation remained, and we agreed to resolve them all.' The only request that Pennar made was to relent on personal guarantees. Litigation was to the tune of Rs 5 crore and was eventually settled.

Back in his conference room and in discussions with colleagues that included Bhaskara Rao, Sabharwal and other trusted old hands, Rao began plans to revive the group. The first step was to identify loss-making ventures and separate profitable ones. As Rao would say, 'We had ridden into the valley of death. Now it was time to ride out of that valley.'

Pennar's board took a call to shelve the refinery project because the investment required was beyond what it had expected and would be a major issue, given the way things were unravelling with other ventures. However, there was a silver lining of sorts, as Nagarjuna wanted to move out of steels and deeper into chemicals and fertilizers.

K.S. Raju and his wife would go to Rao's home and, over dinner, have a discussion that led to an offer to buy the refinery company where Field Marshal Sam Manekshaw was chairman. Raju also offered to buy out the shares of Kuwait investors.

Rao added, 'I took the chairman for dinner one day and explained how the deal structure would work, and after due process, I accepted the offer the Kuwaitis were paid. Nagarjuna bought my shares and my board membership ended. The lands were transferred to the new company where Tamil Nadu Industries Development Corporation was also involved.'

The oil refinery project had synergies for them, so after deliberation, discussion and negotiation, Pennar sold this business to the Nagarjuna group in a swap for their steel business. The Pennar group had clearly identified Pennar Steels as their cash cow and flagship business.

In 1997, the Pennar Group merged Nagarjuna Steel (which was no longer a focus for the Nagarjuna Group) with Pennar Steels through a cashless sharing agreement. By 1999, Pennar Paterson Securities went into liquidation.

It was not exactly smooth sailing after that. Pennar Steels went through its own cycles of birth and death before emerging in a profitable and efficient avatar.

Looking back, was it a mistake to diversify so much? Back in the 1980s and earlier, playing in businesses outside of one's core competence was not just par for the course but also a must-do—and had clicked for many entrepreneurs.

Step by evolutionary step, Rao was finding out that running a business bequeathed wisdom and experience to those in charge, similar to the lessons drawn from spirituality. Also, as he had said himself many times, at least initially for entrepreneurs, 'manufacturing was a bed of thorns, not roses.'

# 8

# The River Bends and Turns but Does Not Run Dry

WHAT WOULD TRANSPIRE NEXT WAS GOING BACK TO THE planning board, a blueprint for a merger with Nagarjuna and one other very difficult task for any entrepreneur: that of downsizing.

By the time the nineties were winding down, Rao had seen the debacle with aluminium severely impact Pennar. While the losses from the venture were one pressure point impacting the group, he found to his dismay, that this was not the only problem. Even as Chinese and Korean imports were one problem for the aluminium business, there was growing competition in the steels business back at home, causing the profit margins and revenue to shrink.

While Pennar checked all the right boxes—getting ISO 9002 certification, tie-ups with technology leaders and rolling out high-margin steel products—the market was becoming difficult to profit from. According to Rao's management, almost 70 per cent of production was cold rolling steel strips or CRSS, which sold for some Rs 22,000 a ton. Those prices kept crashing in a market flooded with cheap steel strips from Russia, Ukraine and Korea. To drum up sales, Pennar made the mistake of dropping prices and offering customers easier credit terms, which led to losses. What made their position weaker was that the steel major, Tata Iron & Steel Company, TISCO, had entered the CRSS market with a giant mill, prices around 7 per cent lower than Pennar's—and they allowed sixty days of credit.

Bhushan Steel, the other big rival, had priced their products marginally higher (2 per cent) than Pennar but allowed 120 days' credit. Pennar's own finance company had folded sometime around 1999, making cheap finance difficult. This was vital given that banks and other lenders had started to avoid borrowers in the steel trade.

Built in the district of Isnapur, which was some 40 kilometres from Hyderabad, PSL started commercial production around 1988. By around 1989, the factory had achieved maximum capacity utilization, generated a profit and declared dividends. The factory had an annual production capacity of 36,000 tons, and within a few years (1995), that capacity was boosted to 60,000 tons a year. Sales and revenue also saw steady growth between 1990 and 1996.

A detailed case study done in 2004 by IIM-Ahmedabad, in collaboration with Rao and his team, gives some context to

Pennar's achievements. The case study looked at Nagarjuna Steel, which had been set up in Patancheru (about fifteen kilometres from Isnapur) in the mid-seventies. By 1995, the plant had a production capacity of 72,000 tons of CRSS and 30,000 tons of cold rolled formed profiles.

While it had officially started much earlier, even under Rao, the Pennar Group took on a much more substantial form and shape when it underwent a merger of sorts with a division that belonged to none other than Rao's former colleague Raju and the company that he had built—Nagarjuna. Pennar Steels and Nagarjuna Steel were both located in Hyderabad and both made CRSS that is commonly used for household appliances, furniture, lockers and filing cabinets.

By early 2000, despite Rao's best efforts, Pennar's financial position started to plummet. On a turnover of Rs 240 crore, it made a small loss of Rs 1.2 crore. However, as the months passed, those losses mounted while turnover fell. By the start of summer in 2000, it was clear that most of the receivables stated in the earlier annual reports would not happen and that the losses would cross Rs 10 crore by December. That was a starkly different story from 1997 when the company had reported a profit of almost Rs 6 crore on a turnover of Rs 115 crore.

Now, with the slowing down in business, the staff and workers had become redundant, and their fixed salaries were depleting the firm's finances.

Before the merger, Nagarjuna Steel had 486 workers, while PSL had 175. The idea of the merger came up in part because of increased domestic competition coming from large players like Bhushan Steel Strips and the hope that with Nagarjuna's added capacity, PSL would become one of the leading CRSS producers nationally.

While CRSS was profitable, Rao was of the view that a merger would allow him to embark on a more sophisticated approach that would enable the forward integration of steel strips in parts such as pre-engineered building systems, auto components, compressor shells, space frames, guard rails and prefabricated shelters. According to his calculations, the margin on these items was 60 to 80 per cent more than on the plain vanilla CRSS products.

The cost of payroll for Pennar was around Rs 90 lakh a month, and the collective thinking was to slash it down by at least half in a bid to conserve funds and ensure the survival of the firm. However, because the company was being pummelled against the ropes across businesses, it made it hard for Pennar to award generous packages to employees who would be required to be laid off, creating a sort of unexpected Catch-22 situation.

According to the IIM case study, Rao's standing instructions were that workers had to be treated humanely and that he could live with losses but not unjust treatment of those who had once worked for him. Over the years, the workers had come to trust Rao and saw him as one of their own. In some ways, a poor send-off was going to be harder for him to deal with than them.

While the merger between Nagarjuna and Pennar created a bedrock of stability, it also meant cutback of staff or retrenchment or layoffs. 'One of the conditions of the swap that K.V.K. Raju's son (K.V.S. Raju) had requested, was for a painless, seamless reorganization and to ensure no local sentiment was hurt,' recollects S.V. Ramachandra Rao, who was one of the earlier hires at Pennar.

When Nagarjuna's Raju was restructuring his businesses, he had certain principles in mind. Like many business houses in the South, Nagarjuna's ventures were built on the back of a workforce from Raju's own village of Bhimavaram. That also meant it was going to be hard for him to retrench staff, some of whom may have been related to him.

After all, it had always been one of the primary drivers for Rao to generate employment. His priority was to create an organization that could provide livelihood for the largest number of workers. And the culture at Pennar was created with that view. The family day functions at Pennar, which were held on Republic Day, were major events of particular significance to him. All the workers of the company along with their families would attend the functions. The atmosphere was festive, with employees and family members all participating in games, musical and sporting events, esoteric contests of skills and awards for accomplishments. The family days also became forums where the management and the workers of the company—typically living separate work lives and working largely independent of each other—could interact as colleagues, thereby allowing for an open forum for association, attended by thousands every year.

Rao recalls having multiple meetings with his team, board and advisors, but try as he might, he could not find a way to continue running the company unless he laid off a substantial portion of his labour force—and permanently.

Rao initiated the harshest cost-cutting measures in the life of the company, and his own for that matter. Every member of the top management ended up taking a voluntary pay cut of 15 per cent. Rao's two key executive assistants—Rajnikant Punjala and Sunil Kurram—also took a step back. Kurram, who was more involved with Pennar Finance, took a break for six months and took courses in IT, while Punjala resigned and left to go work for a company run by Rao's son-in-law.

All activities that were deemed to be marketing or public relations driven were withdrawn. Celebratory occasions, functions and parties, including the annual one to which employees came with their families, were scrapped. Corporate entitlements to business class travel and premium accommodation were now cut back. Executives were asked to fly budget when needed and stay at three-star hotels and guest houses.

The IIM case study says that business consultants Deloitte Haskins & Sells, who had been roped in to help reset Pennar's strategy, pointed to overdependence on the low-margin CRSS steel and the high cost of finance as core reasons for the company's slipping finances. They suggested getting rid of the Isnapur plant in toto and using the funds to pay off existing debts to lenders. But that was easier said than done because there were no buyers for a factory that made low-value steel. Instead, what Rao did was this. He got the management to shut it down in January 2001. The staff and workers were made to report at the Patancheru plant, where shifts had been reduced. Workers did not like the plan, but it was the only course of action available.

Of course, there was another challenge with this new strategy as well. With the transfer of the Isnapur workers, the Patancheru plant was suddenly, but not surprisingly, overcrowded. There were 325 workers, where 150 were required. The management pulled out 175 workers at random and put them in an air-cooled shed stocked with newspapers and refreshments. The plant was run with the remaining 150 workers.

In due course, the workers who were not being used got the idea that they were not needed, and for those who did not, salaries were delayed by a couple of months. The writing was on the wall and they all read it clearly enough.

Later that year, according to company records, Pennar sent a formal, written application under the Industrial Disputes Act, 1947, to the Labour Commissioner to retrench over 200 redundant workers. One copy of the application was handed over to the unions, and another was displayed on the plant notice board. The unions, however, continued to tell workers that their jobs would be secure and that it was unlikely permission for such a retrenchment would be given by the commissioner. That tussle would continue, with the hapless workers going back and forth between the official statements issued by management and the conflicting guidance given by the unions.

Meanwhile, Pennar's senior HR team had started chalking out a Voluntary Retirement Scheme (VRS) plan for the batch of workers that were to be retrenched. The new plan, according to the IIM case study, was to offer the redundant workers thirty days' wages (as against the statutory minimum retrenchment compensation of fifteen days' wages) for every completed year of service besides the standard retirement benefits such as gratuity.

There was an internal back and forth on that as well. Given that Pennar had already run up losses of over Rs 10 crore and was expecting at least Rs 50 crore in losses by the end of the financial year, the company would be stretched to be able to raise the Rs 2 crore needed for the severance package.

A group of senior execs banded together and requested Rao to cut the compensation to the legal minimum. Rao disagreed and pushed back, saying that his workers were not corporate white-collar execs and they would need the extra cash. It was imperative they get more than just what was legally mandated and he urged them to see where they could sweat out more funds for that.

Even though it was not formally announced, by early 2001, the unions, as well as the workers, knew of the company's plans for a stripped-down VRS. Bhushan, Rao's childhood friend who had come on board to run external affairs and public relations, says that happened because of the close community relations between the workers and managers, regardless of designation. Many came from the same village and were of the same sub-sects within Telangana or Andhra Pradesh.

The VRS package was not something the workers wanted to accept. Sure, they were aware that salaries were being delayed almost every month, and many of them were ready to jump ship. But they wanted a VRS package that was a repeat of what was handed out earlier in 1998 when employees were retrenched. The 1998 retrenchment occurred during the Pennar-Nagarjuna merger, and the terms then were more than generous: gratuity plus six times the statutory minimum retrenchment compensation. Workers who accepted it got an average of almost Rs 2,50,000 in addition to around Rs 60,000 towards gratuity.

Back then, far more workers applied for the VRS than the number to be let go. That is what the workers wanted in 2001, but given Pennar's cash crunch, there was no way this could be fiscally possible. It looked as if Pennar was headed for a protracted deadlock with its workforce. The workers, guided by their unions, had decided that they would settle for nothing less than two months of severance pay.

However, in a few months, the workers lost faith in the three different unions that worked with Pennar. Alarmed and dismayed, they turned to the one man who, they hoped, would offer them some clarity—Rao. So, for the next two months, as Rao recalls, groups of a dozen workmen each met him in batches for long-drawn-out meetings. In addition, another five groups of staff who were classified as redundant also met Rao, despite his top management advising him against this.

Most who knew Rao were not surprised by that reaction.

In many ways, it was, after all, his raison d'être to create more jobs and employment as well as grow India's industrial landscape.

V. Rangaraj, who was the founder chairman of the US India Importers Council and worked with Rao at close quarters when he was president at the Indo American Chamber, said that when he was nominated as national president, he was all about pushing for growth in India and in bolstering strategic ties with America corporations. His key focus was on healthcare and education, and at one point, he wanted to kick off a healthcare business that was built on the model of the Massachusetts General Hospital. 'How will you have a good workforce unless they are healthy and educated?' Rao had asked. That idea was eventually executed and rolled out by the Hindujas.

---

There are two classic theories of leadership style, according to American management thinker and professor Douglas McGregor—Theory X and Theory Y. According to McGregor, Theory X assumes that people dislike work and must be coerced, controlled and guided to their organizational goals. Also, most people prefer to be treated this way to avoid responsibility.

Theory Y involves the synthesis of goals and focuses on the average person's intrinsic interest in his work, his aim to be self-directing and to seek responsibility, as well as the capacity to be creative in solving business problems. Rao was undoubtedly a Theory Y CEO.

His own experiences, principles and beliefs being the reason why he would not give up. Rao was clear about one thing: he would never be a leader who was going to duck for cover when the going got tough. So, he did what he knew how to do best, as he had always done—kept his office doors open, faced the hard questions and gave his workers the honest answers. Those who recall that time say that it was not easy on Rao. At what is known as the 'VRS sessions', several staff and workers had emotional meltdowns that resulted in tears. The future for any blue-collar worker and even a white-collar employee was uncertain. The job market was stagnant, and they were fearful of how they were going to take care of their families.

As empathetic as Rao was by managerial DNA, he was equally sincere and direct. 'There is not much I can promise you here at Pennar, and my best wishes are with you. I advise that you look for better jobs, and we will support you with recommendations and referrals where possible, but we cannot guarantee a placement.'

The reactions were varied and ranged from quiet resignation to silent disappointment to a few cases of abusive outbursts. There was, however, no violence, and through it all, Rao gritted his teeth and soldiered on, even though morale was at rock bottom.

Despite Rao meeting everyone and answering their queries, not everyone agreed to leave. A clique of workers continued to insist on a replay of the terms of the 1998 package as a condition for leaving. As is the case in Indian companies, especially in an industrial environment, they were aware that they could not be terminated overnight. The legal system was not a proponent of such action and was prone to treating the right to employment as more fundamental than clauses on a contract that a worker may have signed with or without duress. Of course, the employees also knew that they did not have the protection that certain unionized workers had.

The tug of war continued and involved many, many meetings between Rao and his team and the workers and the unions. Finally, realizing the truth with regards to Pennar's finances, workers started to sign up under the new VRS offer despite unions remaining opposed. 'Behind closed doors, the unions were well aware of the hard times that Pennar was up against but could not support it openly because of their political stand,' recalls T. Rama Rao, HR Head of Pennar.

Rao went the extra mile and reached out to all his workers directly with notices in Telugu, simple and direct, and by doing so, bypassed the unions. The translated version said:

> Dear Pennar Operatives,
>
> Pennar Industries has been in a crisis for a year as there is not enough demand for its products and because it is unable to compete with big companies like Tata Iron and Steel Company. Last year, the production level of CRSS went down from 8,000 tons a month to 2,000 tons a month. Owing to this, the production at the

Patancheru unit had to be stopped. In the financial year 2000–01, there was a loss of Rs 35 crore [350 million]. The situation is such that we cannot provide work for almost 200 operatives and many staff members, and we are not able to retain staff other than the essential ones.

In this scenario we are constrained to lay-off and retrench about 200 operatives. While retrenchment is for the least experienced employees, those with more experience will get an opportunity to leave under a Voluntary Retirement Scheme.

The Voluntary Retirement Scheme, released today (20 April 2001), will be in force till 30 April 2001. This does not mean that the notices issued by management in February with regard to lay-off and retrenchment are cancelled. Those notices will continue to be in force to the extent necessary to control the number of operatives.

Operatives taking the Voluntary Retirement Scheme will get the following payments:

1. Earned Leave Salary.
2. Gratuity
3. Thirty days' salary for each completed year of service as compensation (a total sum of basic, fixed D.A. [Dearness Allowance], and variable D.A. will be considered as salary). A minimum of Rs 40,000 will be paid as compensation.
4. LTA [Leave Travel Allowance] due.

> The full details of the scheme have been released through the VRS notice. Applications for VRS will be accepted based only on the terms and conditions mentioned in the Scheme. Our objective in writing this letter to you is to make you aware of the company's position. We ask you to see for yourselves all the pros and cons of the scheme and take appropriate decisions yourselves.

It had a serious impact and made all the difference. There was also a general congregation held where the workers were told that if they did not follow the suggestion on retirement, there would be no Pennar factory left and the company would essentially shut down. To hear those who were there talk about it, Rao was almost ready to walk the talk and close shop if required.

Finally, redundant workers accepted the VRS offer, and everyone could breathe easy. Even workers charged with indiscipline applied for VRS. Pennar withdrew charges and allowed them VRS benefits. In the end, all the resignation went off smoothly and without any violence or untoward incident.

On 2 May 2001, the company let 212 workers go under VRS.

In retrospect, could there have been any way to avoid the lay-offs?

Ram Koteswara Rao, who was a union head and worked with Pennar, said that the hard-as-nails truthful answer was 'no'. He went on to say that production had crashed from 8,000 tons a month to 2,000 tons. Peer group competitors that included Bhushan and TISCO (Tata Iron & Steel Company) were big, strong and had deep pockets. In addition, he added that they also had newer and more cutting-edge technology at that point in time. Pennar, meanwhile, had notched up debts of around Rs 180 crore that had to be paid back to its lenders.

Rao and the management had rolled out the action of retrenchment not to increase profits but to ensure Pennar's survival. Koteswara Rao went on to emphasize that every single worker knew both the company's financial position and production situation. 'They also knew how well they had been looked after when the company was doing well,' he said.

In a sense, despite the blow to his ego and his company's finances, the Y Theory leader had triumphed. In total, Pennar would ultimately end up paying close to Rs 10 crore from its reserves to workers by way of VRS compensation.

Bhushan recalled that by the time Pennar Oil had been disposed of and Rao was done with the messy matter of shutting down Pennar Paterson, he was more or less done with the worst of the business cycle in his company. 'He was definitely disturbed that he was unable to employ as many people as he wanted to and instead had to actually let people go,' he recalls.

Bhushan adds that the merger went through as smoothly as it could in those times, and some of the learnings that Rao had harnessed from his entrepreneurial life in resolving labour, market and debt issues were also about what not to do.

# 9

# Coming Back to Life: Distressed Debt, the Turnaround and a New Game Plan

Aditya Rao, Nrupender Rao's son, was in the middle of his junior year at Cornell University in Ithaca, New York, when he received the news. His parents had been in a violent and dangerous car accident in rural Andhra Pradesh en route to a wedding for the nephew of his mother, Rajyalakshmi Rao.

The wedding celebrations were being held in Eluru, a town in West Godavari district.

Nrupender and Rajyalakshmi Rao and a couple of relatives were in a Hyundai Accent, driving towards Eluru from Kakinada. They had been staying with relatives in Kakinada, the capital of East Godavari district. Eluru was not too far from Kakinada, so the Raos decided to leave Kakinada in the evening. It was 31 January 2004. Rao, his wife, her father, and a driver got into the Accent, a sedan that is more known for its design and economy than for ruggedness or toughness. Rajah Inuganti Chinna Rao chose to ride shotgun beside the driver, and the Accent joined a small convoy of vehicles heading to Eluru for the wedding festivities.

Talking about that evening, Rajyalakshmi Rao says, it was perhaps an inexperienced driver or a dangerous bend in the road, or a combination of the two that resulted in tragedy. Whatever the reason, the car, which was travelling at a relatively safe speed of sixty kilometres per hour, rammed into a large commercial vehicle that had broken down and had been left on the road without any lights switched on.

The impact of the collision killed Rajah Inuganti Chinna Rao on the spot. The passengers in the rear seat fared just a tad better; they did not lose their lives, but suffered serious injuries. Rajyalakshmi had extensive facial fractures and cranial injuries and fractures in her right arm, leg and ribs, and Nrupender Rao hurt his head. Luckily, the entourage of friends and relatives who were in other cars behind the Accent instantly swung into action.

The Raos were whisked off to Eluru Government Hospital as the accident happened closer to the town where the marriage was to take place and were there quickly. The doctors asked them to shift to a larger hospital in a bigger city, and they were then taken to Hope Hospital in Vijayawada.

Family members recall that the doctors in Vijayawada concentrated on treating Rao's wife more than him as he had no visible injuries. They advised surgery and plastic surgery for her since she had a broken arm and multiple fractures on her face. They were then brought to Hyderabad after initial medication and admitted to Apollo Hospitals, where surgeries were performed on her. Rao's problem was diagnosed only when he went to Kakinada where he fainted ten days later when he went to attend his father-in-law's ceremonies. When he was admitted to Apollo again, Rao underwent brain screening and the scans showed clots in the brain. He underwent a significant midline shift of his brain as well as an epidural hematoma. The last is when there is bleeding between the brain and the skull, and it can be a life-threatening condition or cause brain damage if left untreated. Most important, treatment must be immediate. That was when the burr hole surgery was performed. A surgeon used 'burr hole' surgery, a serious and invasive procedure for draining the blood from the skull to relieve the pressure on the brain immediately.

Rajyalakshmi Rao was slowly emerging from the shock of the accident. Her indefatigable spirit came through yet again. Unlike the soft cotton sarees that she liked so much, Rajyalakshmi had the strength of pure steel. In many ways, she was the rivet that kept the family together.

Even as she dealt with the trauma of losing her father and the pain of her own injuries, Rajyalakshmi steeled herself to be strong for her children and her seriously injured husband. Her role in supporting the family, especially at this time of crisis, cannot ever be overestimated.

Traditional enough to be the last to eat during family sit-downs yet modern enough to override any opinions when it came down to it, Aditya recalls that no matter what happened, she maintained an even keel; her composure, says her son, was in part laced with humour and in part infused with hope. The optimist in her was sure they would beat all odds.

Through his hospitalization, she was by Rao's side, telling him things would be alright, things would get better. She encouraged him to believe in his own strength to overcome this crisis too. Then she would distract him, asking if he remembered this person or that from the past. For instance, did he remember Ramachandra Raju, a former employee at Pennar who was present during the Pennar Aluminium years?

If Rao was warm, friendly and trusting to a fault, then his wife was the perfect foil, being the eternal stoic, as tough as nails, and always ready to take on challenges. She was the proverbial glue that kept the clan together. Raju does not get into details but said that she could also be tough and uncompromising when needed, likely referring to difficult employees, influencing the hard calls that maybe Rao was slower to talk about and exhibiting the sharper point of view on family matters.

Rajyalakshmi was also the reason the children were brought up in a value-based environment. They were not typical entitled rich kids; they were brought up to be humble and polite to everyone, whether it was staff at home or peers.

In essence, the next generation, while worried, was reassured that their parents would pull through the accident and make it through in one piece, even though the damage done to Rao was far more severe, potentially even in the long term.

Dr Surender Rao, a medical doctor and former head of a corporate hospital in Andhra Pradesh, and who also happened to be Aditya's father-in-law, remarked that after the accident, Rao was put on powerful anti-epileptic medicating drugs. 'What they did was that they prevented convulsions and any long-lasting side effects that may have been anticipated. To be clear, they worked and did the job just fine from what we could tell,' he says. 'He [Nrupender Rao] was never one to stress about anything beyond a point anyway and dealt with the whole incident extremely courageously.'

With all this going on, Rao's faith and beliefs in the spiritual never wavered. Rao's faith and spirituality helped him cope with this challenge too, as he has always found strength in his spirituality whenever he faced difficulties. In the earlier years as well, he flew to Calcutta, stayed at the Taj Bengal, and then travelled early morning by car to Belur Math.

Belur Math was rife with history. Sometime around 1897, the history books suggest that Swami Vivekananda arrived in Bengal. There with a small but loyal coterie of followers from the West, he proceeded to establish twin monasteries: one at Belur, the headquarters of the Ramakrishna Mission and the other, called the Advaita Ashrama, at Mayavati in Uttarakhand, nestled in the Himalayas. The objective of these monasteries was to receive and train young men who would eventually become monks of the Ramakrishna Mission.

Belur Math, which became the headquarters of the Ramakrishna Mission, was not far from the Kali Temple in Dakshineshwar and, as a structure, came to symbolize the very heart of the Ramakrishna movement. Its architecture, expectedly, was infused with Islamic, Hindu, Christian and Buddhist designs as a reflection of the underlying unity of man and religion.

Rao was surprised to see how many devotees would attend the initiations. He made sure to visit all the temples, especially the ones for Ramakrishna and Vivekananda and the Holy Mother. Later, he drove down to Dakshineshwar, where he visited the Shivalinga and Radhakantha temples. It was a spiritual journey that was deeply personal. In many ways, Rao felt he was stepping back in time to see what his spiritual leaders were experiencing. He made it a point to go to the Ramakrishna room, where Ramakrishna is said to have prayed. Later, he also went to the room where Swami Vivekananda stayed, praying there, absorbing the spirit of the faith established by those two men decades before.

He ended the trip with a visit to Advaita Ashrama, established in March 1899. It was set up by Vivekananda and disciples James Henry Sevier and Charlotte Sevier and published the original writings of Vivekananda. As a monastic centre dedicated to the study and practice of Advaita Vedanta, it does not permit idolatry. There were no images or idols there, not even of Ramakrishna. There was no luxury there, either. There were vegetable gardens, cold water baths and early morning discourses over hot tea. The visit was around a year after the accident.

---

Even as the road accident disrupted the tenor of Rao's life, he did not allow it to disrupt his work. He came back with renewed energy to get Pennar back to speed. In 2016, he assumed the chairmanship of CII Telangana and under his stewardship, worked on improving the ease of doing business. According to the DIPP, the state was ranked topmost in the country for ease of business, as well as played an active role in various committees that included labour welfare, minimum wage advisory board and single window clearance. But the accident also may have given him some intimations of mortality, and he began to plant the seeds of succession and a generational transition.

At Pennar, he took pains to motivate employees with words that inspired him. He would reiterate that manufacturing was not romantic like a flower bed, but it was like a garden of thorns. When every single thorn was removed, the flower garden would emerge.

It was Napoleon who is supposed to have said that a leader is a dealer in hope. This is exactly what Rao was—to his team, his management, and to his son, Aditya.

His next generation of leaders was growing up but perhaps not yet fully ready to take the reins from him. Rao knew there was a lot more he had to do to ensure that Pennar would see a resurgence of its business fitness and get into a position that would enable its handover. Rao reflected on the challenges that lay ahead of him. His style of personalized business had been so different back in the day. He would know every sweeper, every driver, every single factory shop worker by first name.

The next generation of leaders would sooner or later come into their own and have to contend with new ways of working. There were more machines, more automation, more robotics, and much more competition. Earlier it was the norm for workers to stick around at a company for twenty or thirty years; now, and in the future, it was getting to be transient and more transactional. Rao's mind drifted to *Future Shock*, the book on disruptive life, written by American futurist and author Alvin Toffler in 1970. The book, an international bestseller, talked about how society was undergoing massive structural changes. It would go through a revolution from an industrial society to a 'super-industrial society' with a hyper-accelerated rate of technological and social change. How would that leave people? Pennar's leadership at that point would have to figure it out for themselves, he reflected. For now, his immediate task was to turn Pennar around.

But what had happened to the business to demand a turnaround? Simply put, the group, whose turnover was at around Rs 76 crore in 2002, had found itself referred to BIFR or the Board of Industrial and Financial Restructuring in 2003. That was after the debacle with aluminium, and the overall downturn in metals at large, had led the business to nosedive, suffer huge losses and see margin pressure on profits between

1998 and 2002. From a robust and healthy Rs 320 crore of sales in 1998, revenue was down by more than 75 per cent to Rs 76 crore in 2003.

The same year, in 2004, the corporate debt restructuring forum or CDR cleared a scheme that would let Pennar slash its long-term debt from Rs 245 crore to Rs 185 crore by 2005. The plan was created by global consulting firm Deloitte and included a number of initiatives to help Pennar make the pivot. That included opening new product and business segments and increasing focus on exports. The gamechanger and thrust was to be zeroing in on business for the railways. Pennar already made products for the railways, including high-strength tensile steel and billets and coach metal.

Yet Rao, at least externally, never showed any sign of despondency or giving up. In private, according to his friends and family, he was becoming more and more withdrawn, and while he never lost the light in his eyes, there was a sense of aloofness that had crept into his demeanour.

Where was he going to get the capital to execute the turnaround? He initiated conversations with a string of banks and investors and was finally in an advanced stage of a conversation with an investment arm of a foreign bank when he got a call from a specialist company called Eight Capital Group. Eight Capital was an investment firm founded in 2005 by two brothers, Ravi and Vikram Chachra.

Their primary focus lay in investing in distressed debt and special situation investments in India. The company counted as its expertise the ability to turn around stressed companies through balance sheet restructuring and the organizing of turnaround capital to bring back growth. There was also another common denominator between Ravi Chachra and Rao.

Decades ago, Chachra's Jamshedpur-based family ran a company that manufactured mopeds. Rao had actually been on the board of that company in the 1980s for a short while because of his background in steel and also because Chachra's uncle was in the same batch as him at IIT.

Ravi Chachra called up Rao after getting his number from his uncle and set up a meeting.

Of course, Rao did not remember the nephews from those days, but he did meet them—and decided to keep an open mind. Chachra, who had visited dozens of distressed companies in a bid to find a target that warranted turnaround, saw something special about Pennar when he started analysing its operations. Pennar, at the time, was EBITDA positive but with low single-digit margins and some Rs 400 crore in revenue. That gave the Chachras some comfort.

Chachra, who got his business degree at Wharton University and worked on Wall Street, had launched his firm with investments from JP Morgan. In a short period of time, he had visited 160 distressed companies and went on to invest in some eleven operators. Never once did he think Pennar was distressed when he checked out its facilities. 'When I walked into their factories, everything had a fresh coat of paint. The floors were being vacuumed and the machinery cleaned and polished,' he recalls. It struck him as unusual, and when he asked Rao what that was all about, he was told that because capacity utilization had been so low, what the management had done was tell the workers to paint the facilities and clean stuff up. 'We gave them a pail of paint and said go to work and be productive,' Rao had told Chachra. Paint was cheap, but new facilities kept everyone active—and morale buoyant. 'It was clearly a very proud team at work there,' Chachra recalls. 'You could eat off the floors there—it was the cleanest place I had ever seen.'

Chachra immediately recounted a case study he had learnt about when in business school and which involved the aluminium giant Alcoa. It was a story about the Alcoa turnaround. What the executive in charge had done was ask the teams to show him an accident report. He used that report to drive sweeping changes across the organization that rippled into operations research, greater manufacturing efficiency and so on. Chachra saw similar signs at Pennar, and as his confidence grew, he did the due diligence that he did at most companies and which usually took a hundred days to complete.

While the deal was essentially to shoulder the debt that Pennar had run into, it would involve Rao giving up equity as well. Chachra says that in exchange for taking on their debt of around Rs 150 crore, Pennar was to take on over Rs 100 crore in debt and about Rs 20 crore in equity for cash, which would bring their stake down to about 38 per cent from 45 per cent. Eight Capital would later up their stake to almost 26 per cent. The deal gave Pennar an additional Rs 20 crore to set up a factory for boxes for railway containers in Chennai, a very high margin business. Pennar had the bare bones to execute—all that they needed was some new machinery, some know-how and the capital to make it all happen.

Chachra was not afraid to get into business with Pennar, given the team he saw, the trust he felt, and also the fact that Rao came across as collaborative and ready to deliver on the terms that were set out. Eight Capital's lawyers were fairly aggressive at one stage, and Rao called Chachra to tell him to tone it down; otherwise, the deal would not happen. In turn, Chachra did give up some covenants in the term sheets but what also gave him confidence was the fact that Pennar agreed to something that most companies do not.

Eight Capital put in an EBITDA covenant, which allowed them to advise on what Pennar did with earnings before interest, and if they did not meet targets, Pennar would have to bring in the shortfall if those projections were not met. In other words, they would have to fund the difference of the shortfall as per a subordinated note. Pennar agreed, and the deal was done in June 2006. Was Eight Capital leery of the deal initially? 'We do have a touch and feel for the cash in the company's system, and typically leakages happen when a player is buying materials from overseas, and there is over-invoicing and funds are being diverted to dollar accounts abroad and the like,' Chachra observed. 'However, with Pennar, all their deals for materials were with large, organized players back home and so everything was there in black and white.'

The other avenue that leads to leakage of funds in a company is when the sales of scrap metal or the commodity in question is sold. Those revenues can sometimes be fairly significant, and many companies do not report them. Pennar, however, was actually holding organized auctions and it was adding to their bottom line. That was an important point given that Eight Capital had actually worked since with another textile player who got their materials from farmers and then whose scrap material was being exported through an agent and the volume accounted for as much as 18 per cent. They did not understand the business, and that was a learning, and they consequently learned to spot for revenue leaks which they did not see at Pennar.

In yet another instance of how companies manoeuvre the system to siphon funds out, Chachra says, one deal involved a cement-maker. Eight Capital did not lose money on that gambit, but they realized that the materials involved were very heavy. Limestone and coal needed dozens of trucks to move goods in and out of factories, and the expenditure was hefty. As it turned out, the network of trucks was owned by the promoters who were charging an extra 5 per cent over the market rates for the same freight. Eight Capital did ask the owners to rationalize the cost and get back to efficient costs, but the point is some promoters do find a way to get one past investors, he says.

The trick to finding the right distressed assets in India is part science and part art. That is because one has to find the companies that cannot cross the chasm for genuine reasons. 'It has to be a good company with high debt on its balance sheet but has products and pricing power, can be turned around and has the promoters and management team with the chops as well as the will to do it,' explains Chachra.

Pennar checked all those boxes as far as Chachra was concerned and it was not just social connectivity driving that view. The loyalty towards Rao from his team was unwavering—and very unusual. Most promoters do not have that kind of support, and what that meant was that Rao was not necessarily the biggest or best industrialist but was seen as doing the right thing. He perhaps fostered feedback quite well and would listen to the experts he would rope in. Many hire the best and then do not listen.

'That Rao is a good listener is one of his key strengths, and he genuinely tries to understand what is being said while most promoters whom we meet do not hear what we are really trying to say,' says Chachra.

Eight Capital gave Pennar thirty-six months to return the cash for the debt they had incurred, and to their pleasant shock and surprise, not only did they go past the EBITDA target that was stated, but they returned the funds within eighteen months. 'It turned out to be the perfect company to invest in,'

Chachra says. Rao never had to be reminded about payments, and there were never any delays in coupon payment; Pennar even prepaid them.

There was a series of steps that allowed for that all to happen.

In the beginning, Pennar had almost 80 per cent of its revenue coming in from cold rolled steel, which, as everyone knew by then, was not the best business to be in. It was low-margin, and the big boys had already entered it, which meant they could not compete beyond a point. Pennar did have about 20 per cent of its business come from value-added steel services. The idea was to then turn around and flip the ratio and grow it to 80 per cent and reduce the more commoditized part of the trade to 20 per cent. The proposal was made to Rao and his board, and luckily for all, they accepted and went after those targets.

One of the value-added businesses was steel tubes. It was not easy to make, as one had to take the seams from the inside out, and they were used as shock absorbers, but Pennar figured it out, even though they started from scratch. It was a high-margin business, and it went well for them. Then the company restructured its organization to make some six different strategic business units that oversaw the railways business, the steel tubes, profiles and so on. The main reason for the SBUs was so that the management could keep an eagle's eye view of the cost of capital and not pull funds out of a kitty to put into another project before getting the entire picture. In effect, the company could then see a report of the P&L at the SBU level and not at the holding-company level.

Because they had also implemented SAP software systems early enough, it helped them to get into that sort of zone of financial visibility.

On the lighter side, when the deal was closed, Rao and Eight Capital officials celebrated at Taj Banjara with a multiple course meal for 120 people. 'He insisted on opening a bottle of wine for a toast even though he did not drink,' Chachra says.

As Pennar grew healthier and stronger, and 2008 rolled along, the world went into an economic downturn spurred on by the Lehman Brothers financial crisis in the US. Chachra suggested to Rao that he could push the envelope a little by buying companies in America that were available for pennies on the dollar. Although Rao was eager, internal consensus was not strong enough to move in that direction.

Pennar's revenue continued to do well and grew as much as four to five times when Eight Capital was working with them. However, one shortfall that reared its head was a scarcity of power. Pennar decided to invest money into building a solar plant because the learnings from making the mounting would be valuable for their budding prefabrication business. That was of value, but the submission made by Eight Capital to the board run by Rao was that it was okay to run and use for a short sell but made more sense to hive off in the short term because thermal was going to be around for a while and not going anywhere as far as they could tell.

'The good thing about Pennar is that it is not run by a board that sat there and ate cashews. They gave us their word that they would sell the plant in due course and as it turned out, by the time it got built, there was sufficient power in the state,' Chachra said. The plant, which was giving them some Rs 20 crore in EBITDA every year through sales to the grid, was sold at the right time. Even better, it was sold for a profit and helped clean up their balance sheets.

Investors typically like it when a company is nimble enough to divest assets that they need to, and Pennar exhibited that with the solar plant.

Eight Capital stayed invested with Pennar between 2006 and 2017 and ended up generating 35 per cent IRR every year on the debt and a little less on the equity. 'I was extremely fortunate and lucky to work with him and help turn the company around, and the main difference with him is that he has ambition with integrity; it is very rare in distressed assets and that he wanted to watch out for all stakeholders,' says Chachra.

By the end of this stint, Pennar had become somewhat like an orchestra. They could make the largest road barriers, cold drawn welded tubes, wagons, coaches and tubes. And if one part of the economy slumped or tanked, it still allowed them to hedge their bets and continue growth in another area. That meant there was continuous growth. The company got better as it got larger and was smart enough to have paid more to acquire better talent and gradually increased their own equity stakeholding as well.

Meanwhile, as far as health went, although Rao had turned a corner, it was evident that he was suffering from some sort of physical impairment. His speech pattern had started to change, and those who knew him well would notice that he was not his normally vibrant self, especially when making presentations.

Chachra observed that despite his condition, he would attend every board meeting, come into every presentation and read up on everything he had access to.

'In my final days at Pennar, he was able to speak but not able to walk well and would show up at every meeting with the help of an aide and then leave,' he said.

---

It later turned out that Rao was fighting a neurological disease that was clinically diagnosed as an upper motor neuron disease called Corticobasal Degeneration (CBD). Rao's family did not have an inkling as to how it got triggered but suspected that it may have been in some small way precipitated by the car accident. It was a hard and uphill battle that Rao would have to fight—and he was going to be alone on this one.

# 10

# A River at High Tide

DRIVE SOME SEVENTY KILOMETRES AWAY FROM Hyderabad city through some of the more verdant swatches of the state, and you will reach an industrial stretch of land. This is where Pennar has its factories and plants located. A walk around any of the factories in this area tells a story of its own. There is Pennar Engineered Building Systems Ltd (PEBS Pennar) factory in Sadasivpet, for instance, where it is unwise to enter without a hard hat. Don a helmet and enter the premises, and you will see long flat plates of steel being cut and sheared into beams and metal structures that are waiting their turn to be shipped out to a multitude of industries. The large, illuminated sheds that stretch for hundreds of metres resemble the sort of workshops in which giant robots are manufactured, à la Hollywood film *Transformers*. In one corner is a yellow dumpster filled with pieces of scrap metal and steel chips.

Guard rails ensure a walking pathway for workers and visitors alike.

Walk to the other end of the plant, and you will see large flat metal columns, painted in white and riveted onto flat bases. They look strong enough to support hundreds of tons in overhead weight. In the near distance, foremen yell orders to their teammates, instructing them on the next steps for the day as trucks pull in and out of the loading and unloading bays.

One has to speak loudly given the din and clanging that heavy metal makes in its industrial birthplace. Several feet ahead, an automated machine that likely weighs several tons glides past. It is a device clearly used for manipulating and moving equipment around the site. Elsewhere, a mechanical arm reaches out to pluck large crates of steel raw material from a commercial vehicle and set them down in a waiting area.

Small crews of men, all clad in helmets, safety jackets, gloves and face shields, move components into roll-forming machines where they are crafted into different shapes. Other workers trade-off doing different jobs from time to time.

Adjoining the steelyard, in another section, is an unusual facility. It more closely resembles a pharmaceutical-grade factory than a hardware one. It is brightly illuminated and spick and span. It is a smaller facility that features neatly lined rows of automated assembly machines, framed, laddered tables and computerized control panels. There is pin-drop silence here as components and flat objects go through an assembly line of sorts before they finally end up in neatly packed six feet by six feet cardboard cartons that are shrink-wrapped and have the words 'Pennar Industries Solar Photovoltaic Modules' stamped on them.

In Sadasivpet's neighbouring Isnapur, you cannot miss a huge signboard that proclaims 'Safety First: Quality. Productivity. Efficiency'. Another sign says, 'Acid Tank 1'. Walking through this facility with its giant boilers, tanks and so on, I am reminded of how we created chemical compounds in the school laboratory—except that the equipment here is a hundred times larger. In another facility, I spy what seems like a square vault the size of a swimming pool is half-buried in the ground. Behind and to the right of it are glass-walled control rooms and the machinery in it seems to be unlike anything I have seen before. There are umpteen security guards around, so I ask what this is about. I am told that certain projects are classified and not open to the public or civilians. I get the message and do a U-turn.

It is impossible to ignore the sheer scale, size and weight of the materials being used in the facilities. Steel, which may be an easy and pliable metal to work with and refashion into products of varying nature, is also no easy metal. Working with steel is hard, heavy and difficult. It requires high temperatures, powerful machines, strong chemicals and specialized step-by-step treatment even in the value-added processes. Today, as modern industry has evolved, the legions of blue-collar workers that once formed the bedrock of labour in the Western world and in India have seen their numbers diminished but not altogether replaced by computerized equipment and control centres. Many workers are not easily visible at the factories, but they are there, busy at work in crane compartments overhead, guiding and overseeing day-to-day functions, as they supervise the assembly of the building blocks of India's buildings, offices, malls and homes.

---

The idea for a new value-added business that would boost both margins and profits came to Rao in myriad ways. Of course, he was always travelling, was well-informed and, therefore, plugged into the goings-on in the world of engineering. More importantly, he had the sense that there had to be smarter ways to build strong, long-lasting structures. It also helped that his son was clued into its usage and applicability in the West and that he sensed it was only a matter of time before it became the norm back home too. That was the birth of the pre-engineered business.

All of that was buoyed by the fact that the group's turnover was back on track. Pennar Industries had reported a turnaround with profits in successive quarters starting April 2004. Turnover reached Rs 647 crore in the twelfth–sixteenth month period ending 2006 with a gross profit of Rs 50 crore and operating profit of Rs 26 crore.

As opposed to building a structure from scratch ground-up, prefabrication begins at a different location earlier than the building site and, in essence, controls construction costs by watching time, materials and labour. Of course, it also requires a collaborative approach with suppliers and developers in regard to the type and size of the units being created.

The technology also created pre-engineered steel and materials as opposed to what is available in the market and is hot rolled, which could not be optimized as easily.

There was also expansion underway, and a new plant for Pennar was being built near PEBS on land in the Velchal village, where there was a railway station nearby. At over a hundred acres, this would become Pennar's largest plant. Specifically, it was on the road from Vikarabad to the Bombay highway, and the land was used for making Pennar wagons and a solar facility. The new plant was inaugurated with a traditional religious ceremony, with a puja at an auspicious time and priests blessing the site in the presence of elders, the locals and the village sarpanch.

Pennar was not only back on its feet, financially speaking, but growing. By 2007, the group had clocked Rs 730 crore in revenue and was growing after the deal with Eight Capital in terms of sales and profits. By 2010, in an interview with financial news channel CNBC TV 18, it was clear that Rao was on to a good thing.

The anchor on primetime announced to viewers, 'The stock and the focus at the moment is Pennar Industries, their subsidiary, the pre-engineered building subsidiary has apparently bagged a big order, we are speaking to Nrupender Rao, the chairman of Pennar Industries. Mr Rao, exactly what is the latest addition to the order book and where does it stand now?'

Rao's answer was: 'Yeah, we recently promoted a subsidiary, Pennar Engineering Building Systems, to make pre-engineered building systems. That plant has gone into production just about three months back and our order book now already stands at Rs 80 crore, and we have bagged orders from some prestigious customers Jindals, JSW, Dr. Reddy's Labs, UltraTech Cement, My Home cements, Core Green Sugars and SBI Power.'

The next question that came at him was: 'In the last three quarters, Mr Rao, your revenues have been around the Rs 180–190 crore mark … Will this subsidiary make a substantial jump or a substantial difference to your revenues and by when?'

To which his response was, 'Yes, now, our main company itself, we have been growing for the last almost three–four years at the rate of something like 15–20 per cent a year, and this year also we expect to grow by an equivalent amount over last year … Next financial year [2010-11], about 15 per cent of the total sales would come from the subsidiary, and slowly, over the course of two-three years, this subsidiary will account for around 33 per cent of the main company.'

The news anchor pressed Rao about the growth plans and prospects. 'Any likelihood of tapping the market for any of your capital expansion plans?' she asked.

Rao shot back: 'Not really.' We actually have a large amount of equity, so we have no plans for going ahead [with tapping the market]. We are actually a company with very low debt; our long-term debt is only about Rs 20 crore. So, we can access debt if we want to, but as of now, we are accessing only our internal accruals, and we are investing close to about Rs 30 crore a year. We are currently expanding our plants at Chennai and at Hyderabad, mainly to cater to the railways. Just to tell you that railway business has become a very important part of our business. For the railway coaches and wagons, we supply steel profiles and the complete superstructure above the chassis, the side walls, the end walls, the roofs, the floor of the railway coaches and also the railway wagons. This year, our railway division turnover would touch something like over Rs 250 crore, and we are looking at over Rs 300 crore for the next financial year.'

By this time, son Aditya Rao had jumped into the business headlong and was assisting his father with more than just divisional duties. He was de facto getting primed to run the group at an overarching level, having completed his education and advanced training and worked at Pennar for a few years in different departments. That was an important inclusion given the way Indian business houses functioned in light of succession challenges—a dynamic that can often lead to disputes, personality clashes as well as contribute to strain on a company.

Rustom Desai, who is a senior lecturer at the Johnson Graduate School of Management and was formerly a global technology executive with Corning Incorporated, says that it is only today that family-promoted businesses are taking the time to develop clear roadmaps around not only succession but also what specific roles the next generation will play in ownership, governance and management (the three pillars that define the role of a family in the company). In that sense, Pennar was ahead of the curve to have started architecting their leadership transition fifteen years ago.

'While it is not appropriate to take names, this trend is very visible in the families that control large publicly traded companies. They are setting up family offices. They are engaging the next generation in the role that it would like to play in the future of the business. They are carving out opportunities for the next generation to have impact early, and to experiment with new ideas.' Desai said. 'They are bringing in professionals in areas where family may either not be interested or capable. All indicators that they are taking succession *and* the future of the business very seriously.'

Desai also emphasized that while the larger companies had started to make their plans for succession, the heart of the Indian family-owned business was still small- to medium-sized privately held companies. 'Mature levels of thoughtfulness and planning were yet to make it to that section of the country.' If Rao had overseas career options available to him for his own charting of career choices, then his son had offshore opportunities, other domestic companies and the family business to factor in.

Desai says, 'The next generation of today's family enterprises are global citizens, and they believe they have choices—whether or not to join the business, and whether or not to be a part of management [versus stay on the governance side only].'

His point is that because their parents understood what direction the business should take, and wanted the next generation to participate, then it was important to create openness towards the next generation's inputs.

'We are no longer talking about millions in dollars of wealth creation, preservation and growth. Large Indian corporations have billions to invest [and worry about]. This is not the kind of asset base that can be managed at the dinner table,' explained Desai.

There were other massive changes afoot as well in big promoter-businesses today as opposed to two decades ago. Technology has created opportunities and threats. 'Who would have thought that in a highly restricted retail space, Seattle-based Amazon would become the biggest retailer in India? Or that a petroleum refiner would be the country's largest telecommunications company that fundamentally disrupts how over a billion people use data, get entertained, and shop?'

Desai went on to explain that twenty years ago, a next-gen leader had one choice: To join the family business in exactly the same form as it was envisioned by the prior generation. 'Today, they could choose to focus on a new business area or enter new markets their parents would not have dreamt of entering. They could choose to hire professionals and play a governance or an executive role,' Desai summarized.

In that vein, Aditya and his father together made progressive decisions. A call was made at an executive level to seek out an overseas partner with expertise in metal pre-engineered building construction.

Desai is not alone in viewing the transition at Pennar favourably. Others see the transition the same way.

Jayant Acharya, director (commercial, marketing and corporate strategy) for JSW Steel, says that while Nrupender

Rao can be credited for setting up the Pennar Group's foundation along with a few of his trusted lieutenants, 'his son Aditya Rao has ably taken over the mantle of responsibility from his father and is leading the company with aplomb. In the last decade and a half, Pennar has become more sophisticated, setting up several verticals which use specialty and high-grade steels, some of which are even supplied by JSW to manufacture products to meet the end-use applications in the infrastructure, construction, general engineering, automotive, white goods and renewable energy segments.'

Eric Brown, an American technology executive in his mid-fifties, has a history of having spent his college and working years in Hawaii, and has worked across sectors and industries, from consulting companies such as KPMG, investment firms and then later NCI Building Systems, which was a maker of prefab equipment—metal products for the construction industry in North America. NCI made products for repair, retrofit and new construction activities. Much later, in 2018, the company went on to be merged with Ply Gem Parent, and the newly formed company proceeded to operate as Cornerstone Building Brands, a $5 billion manufacturer of exterior building products, amongst other things.

For his part, Brown had worked for Wang Laboratories in China and other parts of Asia and was well-acquainted with that part of the world. However, he had never worked for, or with, an Indian company before he worked with Pennar, so he was a little intrigued when a friend of his, who was one of the CEOs at NCI, connected him to the Raos.

'They were quite clear and specific in their objective, which was that they were looking for an expert who understood technology to help them build and design prefab projects,' Brown recalls.

They spoke and decided to go over the idea of setting up a joint venture for that purpose and Rao and his son visited Brown in Houston.

The first thing that Brown was struck by was Rao's humility. 'I had never met a business CEO who was that grounded and down to earth,' he recalls, saying that there was not one single flashy thing about the man he can remember.

In Brown's boardroom, Rao gazed around, seeming surprised that the rooms occupied by senior executives were so much larger than those of other workers. He also seemed taken aback by NCI's private jet and corporate swank, and Brown could tell he thought it was all crazily out of sync with his own experiences and frameworks. 'The funny thing was Rao himself had the resources and background to be comfy with it all,' Brown says. 'That did not mean that he was not on hyperspeed when he was analysing business.'

Even as he gazed at his surroundings, Rao's mind was missing none of the future potential of it all. 'His brain was going a mile a minute and there was this bright sparkle in his eye, the kind of which I had never seen anything like,' says Brown.

Brown would learn that a few years earlier, Aditya had experimented with the idea of a prefab business that had been christened PEBS Pennar, but since the market was not consistent at the time, they had slowed the pace down. The

Raos were now interested in beefing up that company's technical expertise and collaborative strengths.

As Brown got to know Rao, it became evident that he was so concerned about the business and his employees that the line between employees and family was blurred—almost non-existent. 'It was very different from the USA,' Brown says. He later visited the Raos in Hyderabad and was struck afresh by how low-key the family was. The Raos greeted him like he was family, something Brown was not expecting. 'I ended up mentoring his son, and in some ways, I was almost being mentored by Rao like I was his son, so it was interesting in a way.'

Brown would begin working with Pennar on their engineering projects and then later even joined their board as a director. He notes that the culture, in contrast to many Western corporations, was simply not only about the bottom line. 'Sometimes even to their detriment, it seems that just profitability is not the only guiding force.'

What is that driving force, then? Brown would say that it almost felt like the key was knowledge and searching out all the angles in a business. Rao was keen to learn more about figuring out the future opportunities, the higher technology in manufacturing, the new trends and the new practices.

In their projects, the conversations hovered around very specific machinery, 3D printing and how those could be used to make buildings, as well as the usage of robotics instead of manual welding. Brown says the concept was to understand how deployment of technology could work instead of just throwing bodies at a project.

Rao went about hiring the PEBS Pennar senior team in a similar way that he got Brown. The first question Rao asked P.V. Rao, the executive who would help spearhead PEBS Pennar, was if he was interested in coming back to Hyderabad for a while and if the city would suit him professionally.

P.V. Rao, who was originally a native of Vijayawada, had worked in Kuwait for several years on prefab projects and moved on to settle down in Pune when the global recession had kicked in sometime around 2008. A civil engineer by training, he had worked in the Gulf for a range of companies in Oman. He had also worked with Tata Ventures in India with a specialized focus on fabrication and setting up of steel structures. His answer to his future boss was they could discuss it and go over the details, and so they met at the Trident Hotel in Mumbai.

The interview went like this. Nrupender Rao asked how fast the Pune Rao could mobilize a team. Then he asked him about his finances and his family and followed up to emphasize that he would require as many as six different departments, with senior heads, for sales and production levels. Then Rao went left-field and asked him what he thought about human capital. 'He asked me what I thought about the importance of team members and if I was a tough, fighting boss or if I played like a family unit,' P.V. Rao recalls.

By then, the foreign-returned engineer was getting enthused about the prospects of what would have been an interesting stab at an entrepreneurial venture that he could be seen as building from the ground up. The last query he got was, 'Who should drive the business in this niche—finance or HR or project managers or marketing or the engineers?' The answer that Rao got was: 'Sales. Sales should drive the business.' Nrupender Rao could not agree more. 'Yes,' he said, 'indeed, sales has to drive the organization forward, not finance or HR, else it will sink.'

P.V. Rao recalls that Nrupender Rao was looking to check for confidence levels. He was also struck by how trusting a boss Rao was, comparing this with his professional experience in the Middle East where the culture was the opposite. He found this a welcome and refreshing change in terms of leadership style.

It was also a huge opportunity at the time.

---

Aditya Rao, in media interviews, would talk about how there was a billion-dollar market for pre-engineered steel buildings and that the industry was growing by about 15 per cent a year largely because there was also a 4 per cent shift from conventional construction to pre-engineered buildings.

The core team had been set up, orders were flowing in, and PEBS Pennar quickly became amongst the top five players in the country, but they wanted to grow further by revenue and volume of sales. 'We wanted to expand from the current one beamline to two and then three beamlines. A beamline determined the capacity and could allow us to scale up and boost market share,' Aditya says.

So, the company connected with Zephyr Peacock, a PE player in New York, met with their investment team and committee and pitched the plan. Zephyr Peacock did its due diligence roping in KPMG and AZB & Partners to check out the legal as well as the financial parameters for the transaction.

They invested Rs 50 crore and the company, which was valued at around $100 million, listed on the stock exchange in 2017. According to Rao, Zephyr Peacock achieved a three times return in three years, which was very high for the time.

PEBS Pennar would go on to list on the bourses and then execute work that not many had done before in the country.

That included creating a fourteen million square foot building for IOT, which was a JV between Indian Oil Tanking and Oiltanking GmbH, a German company in Dahej. Other efforts included a shed for Aditya Birla that was one kilometre long, a four lakh square feet National Distribution Centre for Reliance Retail, buildings for Ikea, Amazon, Facebook, Mercedes-Benz, Volkswagen and Toyota. PEBS Pennar even made the shell of a seventeen-story building for a developer in Hyderabad within three months.

The long list of marquee projects included aircraft hangars, cold storages, showrooms and sports stadiums.

Eventually, the Raos took a call to make the company private after it hit specific goals. They figured that they did not need two listed companies and that the unit had unlocked the value it needed to, Rao says. 'That business unit has spawned a US entity under Pennar Global, which makes buildings there as well and is one of the most profitable businesses and accounts for a significant percentage of profit.'

The great advantage of the technology, Aditya pointed out, was a saving of around 30 per cent in construction time, which was why P.V. Rao, who was the first employee hired at PEBS, would say that it was profitable from the word go.

The river had turned. The business was back in shape and growing like it was intended, but there were other challenges emerging.

Rao's health was deteriorating. He would have to start using a walking stick and would tell family members with his trademark optimism and courage that he was okay and would bounce back on his own. 'I will be walking on my own soon,' he would tell his family. They, of course, knew that was not going to happen.

In essence, they all knew he was doing what he had learned to do his entire life, which was to be a leader and offer eternal hope to his family, friends and close ones.

# 11

# Running Below the Surface

'My aim was not to merely start a company to make money. I wanted to create an institution, something which would remain and prosper for a long time. Now Aditya, the vice chairman and the president, will have to take Pennar Industries forward. They want to make it a billion-dollar company that is three times the size of what we are today. They want to have a footprint in other parts of the world. A younger team has a better knowledge of the fast-changing world.'

At a Pennar sales meeting a few years ago, Rao made one of his trademark speeches—light-hearted but insightful. It was a typical Rao-style speech designed to encourage performance within the company. Sadly, it was also one of his last speeches at Pennar.

'You can switch on more lights. I have no slides. I am from the older generation, and we generally talk—maybe a lot,' he began with a dash of self-effacing humour.

He went on to say: 'The Pennar Group has something like turnover of Rs 1,500 crore or so and a few board meetings ago when we were in a meeting, I got the board to think a little bit out of the box and told the directors that with other new businesses, I see that we can go up to Rs 2,000 crore, which was half-a-billion dollars at that time. Board members, as well as Aditya, remarked, 'why not a billion-dollar group?'

'At the time, that was beyond my comprehension to be thinking of a billion-dollar group. But with a road map, that can be worked out—this is no longer imaginary and is a goal that every one of you must contribute towards, and make it happen. It will not happen tomorrow and may take five years or even more, but we have the ideas, we have the people and we have the ability to go to market, which is why I feel it can happen.'

Throughout the speech, there was an overriding emphasis on staying humble.

'The only way to get there is to not only meet but actually surpass customer expectations,' Rao said.

He added, 'Ultimately, the purpose of a business is the satisfaction of the customer. Nobody else pays any of your salaries here but the customer. Do not be under that mistaken assumption. Your income comes from customers all over the country, and those are the people who are providing. Therefore, your real master is the customer, nobody else.'

By the time Rao had eased into what could be described as retirement mode induced by his health conditions, the leadership of the group had been seamlessly transferred to Aditya and other management team members. There were a few new members and some old hands who had been with the group for the better part of two decades. The hard years had passed, and the even harder lessons had been learnt by the group. They had taken a new conservative approach in how to tackle business opportunities, assess risk and tackle quick-changing economic environments. The results were obvious. A company that had once struggled with mounting debt, imploding businesses and lender-directed restructuring on account of being unable to pay its loans was now healthy, standing on its own two feet and growing, steadily and with calibration.

The reported standalone quarterly numbers for Pennar Industries for the quarter of June 2021 showed net sales to be at Rs 458.05 crore, up 182 per cent from Rs 162.43 crore in June 2020. Pennar's EBITDA was at Rs 41 crore, up by over 400 per cent from the same time the year before, and its EPS (earnings per share) had increased from Rs 0.53 in June 2022 to Rs 2.36 in June 2022.

At one level, there was no doubt that the company had benefited from its long-standing relationships. Jayant Acharya, director of commercial marketing and corporate strategy and one of the senior leaders at JSW Steel, with $20 billion in market capitalization and one of the largest steel manufacturers in

India, talks about his equation with Pennar with the measured but characteristic precision of a veteran business leader.

For over three decades, he has been immersed in the business of metals and mining and fondly recalls the relationship that he shares with Rao and Pennar Industries, which became one of JSW's first customers almost two decades ago. The relationship between JSW and Pennar and the pivotal role that Rao played in building a mutually beneficial business relationship led to the present foundation of trust and transparency.

The cold rolling and pipe mill that Pennar Industries set up forged a strong alliance with JSW, and together, both the companies evolved as partners to service customers across sectors.

While widespread diversification by business houses was the order of the day at that time, Pennar Industries stood out by concentrating on their core business and focusing on steel and allied steel products. Acharya says that is what held them in good stead to overcome the economic downturn of 2008 and the Lehman crisis. Sticking to what they knew best as a strategy helped them overcome several obstacles in becoming the huge group that it is now.

'One aspect that has always struck us about Pennar is that it has always maintained fiscal prudence in terms of management of working capital and has been conservative in their borrowing without straining their health,' Acharya noted.

He adds, 'As a group, our effort has always been to support Pennar with the best products, services and terms of business.

In business, there are good times and bad times, and we have seen several relationships falling apart and getting strained in the past. However, despite several ups and downs faced by both JSW and Pennar in the last three decades, our partnership has emerged stronger, more resilient and determined,' a quality that speaks volumes of the leadership of Rao.

Acharya also recalls his many interactions with Rao in the past, which would commence with business content for the first few minutes and then Rao would move on to discuss socio-economic issues pertaining to upliftment of people and society at large. Such was his passion and interest to help and be of service to mankind. It is this side of Rao which enabled him to create a company and a team of people in Pennar Industries, which is also known for its huge corporate social responsibility, well before the term became a requirement.

Acharya goes on to note that Rao possessed virtues that are normally not common with many leaders, which is 'a combination of astute business acumen along with a keen understanding of people, benevolence and philanthropy.'

It was something that he also got public acclaim for as evidenced by a number of felicitations that included the Best Entrepreneur Award from the Hyderabad Management Association (HMA), 1994; the Dr Nayudamma Gold Medal for Highest Tax Payer Award from the IT department of Andhra Pradesh, 1995; the Distinguished Alumnus Award for outstanding achievements and contributions from IIT Kharagpur, 2011; the National Award for Outstanding Entrepreneur from Council of State Industrial Development and Investment Corporation of India (COSIDICI), 2013; and the Lifetime Achievement Award from the Hyderabad Management Association in 2017.

Sunil Kuram, who served as Rao's executive assistant for several years and continues to work as a vice president at the group, breaks down that combination in simple terms. For one, he would meet problems head-on as opposed to burying them, only to be tackled later on. 'Bring it to its logical conclusion, else the skeletons will jump out of the cupboard at a later stage,' Kuram says.

Rao exhibited unusual humility by treating both his corporate staff and his factory workers with the same regard and position. 'He would eat in the workers' canteen, and when he would attend employee weddings, he would end up waiting for his driver to finish his meal even if he was done with blessing the newlywed couple.'

The spiritual facet was always in the background, with Rao always giving cash and donations to those who approached him on the birthday of his guru Swami Vivekananda, and he even went as far as naming an early fund after Sri Ramakrishna, Vivekananda and Gandhi. He called it the Raviga Growth Fund.

The sense of inclusiveness extended to his business partners as well. One typical meeting style he developed was the 'sandwich meeting.' Any partner, customer or vendor who would reach out to Pennar for business would have to meet him first, visit factories and meet other heads, and then go back and meet Rao again. That was so that any visitor already had a composite 360-degree view of what they were dealing with when they arrived and, therefore, all parties could potentially be on the same page from the word go.

Most atypical was his ability to inspire employees to dream big for themselves, Kuram observes. His favourite line was always: 'I love it when people tell me they want my position and designation.'

More importantly, unlike many rushed and hurried promoters of today, Rao would always take the time to communicate what his objectives and goals were. 'Communicate and over-communicate,' he would say. 'If the student has not learnt, then the teacher has not taught.'

All these qualities either stemmed from or percolated into his personal life as well. Childhood school and college friend Suresh Kulkarni recalls that he stayed in touch with Rao over the years even after they had grown up and gone the family way. 'As time went on, we continued meeting and talking. I remember providing words of encouragement when he was facing challenges at Pennar. In 2018, I finished writing "Rocket Man", my memoir, and sent him a copy by email,' Kulkarni says. Later in January 2019, he went across to have lunch with him in Hyderabad. By that time, Rao had difficulty walking and talking, but insisted that he would walk to the dining room at the hotel where they would be eating. 'To my surprise, he walked in holding a hard copy of "Rocket Man" in his hands. He pointed to it and gave me a thumbs up. And then he turned to his associate, Sunil, and told him he wanted it to be published as a book.'

Rao, in fact, was instrumental in helping his friend get the book published. In retrospect, Kulkarni says that Rao is a unique person in that he is as brilliant as he is compassionate, and to top it all, he is a leader with a grand idea. 'I remember asking him one time what his goal in life was. He said, "I want to provide employment for over 1,00,000 people and to lift them out of poverty."'

Ironically, while Rao may not have achieved that directly with Pennar, which does employ a few thousand people, indirectly, his efforts did actually achieve those kinds of lofty targets. Remember Manish Sabharwal, the young man he mentored? Sabharwal went on to found TeamLease, which gave (or found) employment to millions of Indians. Incidentally, TeamLease itself has around 2,50,000 employees, accounts for around 5 per cent of the market share of its industry and is amongst the largest staffing companies in the country. Its mantra on its corporate website reads 'Putting India to Work', something that would undoubtedly resonate with Rao.

To get a true understanding of what made Rao so unusual and different from other promoters requires a closer look at how he hired and built his company in the beginning. Former Pennar executive, Pramod Rao, recalls how he had landed an early job and was living in Hyderabad and staying with a friend who worked at Nagarjuna Signode. He had done his B. Com and was around twenty-five years old when he heard that Signode was looking for employees. He met Nrupender Rao, who referred him to the CEO at Signode, Shankar Bhattacharya.

He was consequently sent off after a few meetings within Pennar. Then, some two months later, Rao's secretary called him for a meeting at the Westend Hotel. 'So, I went there,' recalls Pramod Rao. 'When I shared that I had no immediate plans, I was told to come and join him in Hyderabad. There was no interview, no raft of questions.' He was told that his background had already been checked, and given that he had graduated from Rishi Valley School, he would not have any ego, and that worked fine for Pennar.

The Rishi Valley School drew from the philosopher J. Krishnamurti's vision of integrating education into the daily transactions and practices of a school and provided a unique environment that allowed young students to grow not only in intellect but also in other dimensions of their being.

And so, the young Pramod Rao took a bus, went to Pennar's office, and signed on as an executive assistant to Rao. In due course, he became Rao's shadow. His takeaways included some standard best practices: Never keep paper pending on the desk and get it out of the way; do not abdicate but still remain on top of things; and always proofread all communication.

Pramod Rao remembers the one time when the Pennar annual report had been compiled and published. There was a reference to Prime Minister Indira Gandhi with one small spelling error. Gandhi had been spelt as 'Gadhi', which, in Hindi, meant donkey. The young Rao spotted the error and took it to his boss in abject terror of what might happen next. There was no angry rebuke, no rolling of eyes, or exasperation or any emotive outburst. He was simply to find a solution quickly.

Reprinting all the reports was not feasible because there was no time. So, Pramod Rao got just a few copies printed with no errors and made sure that those copies were presented to the Town Hall for the annual general meeting where dignitaries and guests and corporate officials would be in attendance.

'So, you did have the answers and the solutions' was all that his boss said to him about this incident.

Pramod Rao would say of his boss that he was one of those unrecognized management gurus who operated on a no-agenda principle. 'He was way ahead of many management experts even globally, and you would hear that from anyone who worked for him.' Pramod Rao later went on to work in the real estate industry and flourished in his corporate career, working as the chief operating officer for Jerry Rao at his entrepreneurial venture VBHC (Value Budget Housing Company).

Koshy Varghese, an industrial electrical engineer from Kerala who graduated from IIT Chennai, ran into K.V.K. Raju of Nagarjuna, who was visiting faculty there, and the two got along. Raju asked him to work for him at Union Carbide and then later was assigned to the factory in Chennai where Raju was working, circa 1968. A year later, Raju went on to tell him that a new employee called Nrupender Rao was joining and that he would have to go fetch him from the airport. Varghese recalls that he had never met someone as friendly and warm. 'He was simply so pleasant to meet and catch up with and was constantly smiling.'

In due course, Raju kicked off his entrepreneurial venture, Nagarjuna, and Rao was a rising star in Raju's eyes. So, joining the new venture was a no-brainer for both of them. 'Raju was a visionary. Execution was not his strong point, so Rao handled that and became his right-hand man, and I became the man for operations and manufacturing,' Varghese says, adding that there was a shift in the management style and ideology of the group when Raju's son came into the picture.

Varghese went on to join Rao when Pennar started, and after a few years, he chanced upon an executive opportunity in Dubai. It was more lucrative and would give him international exposure, and when he approached Rao with the update, he was concerned that it would be seen as betrayal. Instead, Rao told him, 'This is a God-given opportunity, and you must seize it and join them.'

Varghese was thrown off-balance; at the very least, he expected Rao to show some disappointment. Rao's response made Varghese feel bad about leaving Pennar. 'The thing is he loves all people, workers' union bosses, family … And remember that he had a flair for language, which also helped a lot.'

Rao speaks fluently in English and Hindi, and of course, Telugu. He also has a working sense of Tamil, Bengali and Urdu and a smattering of German. He was a fast reader, consuming as much as 700 to 800 words a minute as compared to the average 200 words a minute for most people, Varghese recalls. He goes on to add that most entrepreneurs are not great managers because the former requires vision and gumption while the latter requires organizational skills and execution. Most do not have both skills, but Rao did.

Ajay Yadagiri, who is Rao's sister's son, grew up in his uncle's house because his parents, who are both doctors, lived away from Hyderabad. He stayed with Rao after the third grade until he finished his course at Nizam's College in Hyderabad. He never worked for his uncle but observed and seemed to notice that he was exceptionally well-read and was the kind of figure that he could approach with any question and get a rational answer. 'He was very goal-oriented and would tell us all to be the best at whatever we were doing. I remember that his eldest daughter, Arathi, had an incentive system. If you got first rank, you would get six books as a reward, second got three and so on.'

The billion-dollar question, of course, that begs to be asked is where did Rao get his drive from, given that he was not incentivized by the usual trappings of fame and fortune? Yadagiri says its roots came from his upbringing; his values came from his father, and his aim was to make things better for everyone. 'In fact, many felt that JVNR was not the best politician because he did not do what most politicians did and instead was driven by uplifting everything around him.'

Not surprisingly, other family members point to a similar approach that was deployed even with his own kin. Sridhar Chelikani, who runs an IT firm in Chicago, says that when he first met his future father-in-law in India over two decades ago, he was taken aback by his friendly yet enquiring approach. He asked Chelikani about his future plans, his aspirations, his interests, and there was a genuine keenness to understand what made him tick. 'I never felt I was being sized up or weighed at any moment, and that geniality ensued throughout the years with him staying in touch and calling and even visiting in the US over regular intervals through the years.' He would visit almost every summer and was the perfect guest in that he was low-maintenance, never had any demands and was always happy with the bare minimum.

Rao and his ability to build and maintain lifelong relationships and friendships went beyond the capabilities of most as his relationships were stronger and nuanced. While most people would remain in touch with perhaps a dozen close friends from their school and college days, Rao would meet every month with a large group of friends from his school and his IIT days all throughout his life. He remained involved in their lives, sometimes even in their careers. Rao had the knack for being able to hold onto most of his friends and all of them became integral parts of each other's lives.

There is no shortage of former employees whose lives Rao helped transform for the better. R.V.S. Ramakrishna first interacted with Rao when he came to the IIM-Ahmedabad campus during placement season. He was interested in hiring talent for the JV that was being set up between Nagarjuna and Signode. 'I was surprised to see a Hyderabad startup coming to campus for hiring. That city in the early eighties was not renowned for commerce and did not have an image for industrialization. There were public sector players and that sort of thing, so this stood out.' He started out as an area sales manager in 1982, which involved marketing and research for the firm.

'From then all the way till now, I see him as a mentor and guide who helped me get started on my corporate journey,' he says. In due course, Ramakrishna became the managing director of the company that by then had changed its name to ITW Signode after Nagarjuna and Rao consequently divested their stakes. Today, it is called Signode India, employs around 1,000 people, and is a Rs 1,400 crore company that makes industrial packaging products with clients that include Tata Steel, JSW, Essar, Vedanta and others.

According to Ramakrishna, Rao was one of the greatest salesmen and not in the used-car manner but in a sincere and effective way that involved strategy and substance. He remembers Rao telling him during his hiring interview that he could have easily joined a large established player, but he would merely be a postman there and that those brands would sell regardless. On the flip side, the challenge that lay in building Signode into a great packaging company from the ground up had learnings that would serve him better and longer. 'I thought I would give it a shot for a few years, and if it did not work out, I could always go back to Mumbai and join a big company, but of course, it did.' Even until a few years ago, the Signode salesmen were considered amongst the top in their category, and that really goes back to Rao in many ways.

Given his insight and astute understanding of companies and workers, why was it that a man with his mindset and IQ was always having to troubleshoot matters? 'I can only say that his trust was total and perhaps that was misused at points of time.' His greatest learning from Rao?

'Trust and delegation are absolutely necessary to motivate teams, but you have to know how to hold the reins, and that is the key. If not, you can lose your revenues and even your company. Chairman Rao went through it all but ensured that he delivered to all his stakeholders to the best of his capabilities.'

You hear things like this at almost every seminar and in every management school, but in terms of practising and execution—that is where the boys are separated from the men.

On a broader scale, business experts could make the argument that had Rao focused on a more business-to-consumer focus area, he may have had even greater success, but business leaders presently still opine that manufacturing and heavy industries will continue to be a core growth engine for the country.

Arun Nanda, who was former executive director of the Mahindra Group and continues to be associated with them in leadership roles, says that while the growing number of unicorns that have emerged in India in the last couple of years and the funds that have been raised both domestically and globally are most welcome, given the size of the Indian economy and the fact that around 50 per cent of its population is young, the real engine of growth will continue to be manufacturing.

'When you look at major economies which grew after the Second World War, including Japan and Germany, it was on the strength of manufacturing industries. Similarly, post the oil crisis, we saw the largest economic growth in China, which was primarily because of it becoming the manufacturing capital of the world,' Nanda says.

There are multiple facts that support Nanda's belief. 'Manufacturing not only creates many more jobs for every rupee spent but also brings multiple other benefits starting with development of technology, the capital expenditure in building the plant and facilities, the distribution networks, logistics and supply chain, suppliers of components and so on. The most important aspect is sustainable development.'

The same applies to traditional services sectors like tourism, hospitality, logistics, etc., because they create more jobs per rupee spent and, more important, indirect employment and investments are several times that of the primary investments. Can you say that for New-Gen e-commerce ventures? As an example, he points to the trending electric vehicle industry, which impacts R&D, design and development, manufacturing facilities, distribution, battery charging stations, service centres, distributors and more. Such heavy industries will help the Indian economy grow consistently and find a huge number of jobs for most of the youth who will enter the working population in the next decade.

'I must add that I am not against the new-age industries as they do bring in investments, both from domestic and international investors, but I believe the real, sustainable growth, coupled with employment, will come from the traditional sectors.' He also stresses that timing-wise, and given the current geopolitical situation, it is opportune for India to focus on manufacturing and related sectors. 'The western world is wanting to reduce their dependence on China, and I do not think any other country is as well placed as India to take advantage of the situation.'

Like Rao professed in his earlier corporate speeches, his philosophy was all about having the self-belief and inherent confidence to be able to succeed no matter what the odds were. 'As a country or as a company, you never approach the market with an inferiority complex that the rest of the field is big and I am small. If you think like that, you are finished on day one,' says Rao.

As the economy and the market developed, Rao warned of increased competition.

'Gone are those days when there was no competition. With liberalization and globalization, we now have competition from inside and outside but remember, we are not around for the short term. We are in it for the long haul. We are a long-distance horse. That also means, in the long run, the truth will emerge, and while you could get away with the untruth for a while, it will not last, so, therefore, keep that in mind, for your work, your personal life and also your country.'

That truth rings eternal.

# Briefly Speaking

*What would you do differently if you could relive your corporate career?*

*Rao:* I regretted taking public depositors for Pennar Patterson.

I believed that a lot of people had placed their hard-earned money in Pennar Patterson because of me, and thus, I felt personally responsible for them losing their money. This thinking led me to ensure resolving all depositor issues. All depositors who approached us were taken care of and got back as much capital as possible.

My attitude on this issue is that this is also why we believe that Pennar Patterson did not face the kind of legal blowback that other NBFCs faced in the nineties. I strongly advised my son never to take public depositor money.

*Your pick from the current crop of business leaders who you think have made the kind of impact that you would have liked to and why, and would like to meet?*

*Rao:* I admire principled and hardworking business leaders. In that vein, I thought highly of Ratan Tata, Narayan Murthy, Azim Premji. I admire founders who are devoted to the ethical and purpose-driven foundational aspects of their businesses rather than a single-minded pursuit of profitability and market capitalization.

*Looking back, are you satisfied with the kind of difference you have made?*

*Rao:* The primary goals in life were to provide employment to 1 lakh employees and to build a lasting engineering- and technology-driven enterprise. While Pennar was able to reach 5,000 direct and indirect employment, I am most proud of Manish Sabharwal and what he had achieved with TeamLease and employment.

I remember when I found out TeamLease had reached 1 lakh employees, I was extremely happy and called Manish immediately to congratulate him. So, in some ways, Manish has taken my dream and made it reality. Even if I did not do it, I am glad he did.

*Your sense of spiritual dedication and belief—is that something you feel gave you the faith to continue your journey in life?*

*Rao:* I am a spiritual person. My belief system was grounded in the importance of first being a good person. The foundation of my drive, ambition and energy lays in the teachings of Swami Vivekananda. Through all the problems I have faced in life, my core strength never wavered, and I believe this continues to give me the strength to fight every challenge I have faced, and to remain positive.

Like Hanuman, every person has infinite strength in them. We do not know our own strengths. If we believe in ourselves and give up our self-doubt, we can overcome even impossible odds.

*Do you have a bucket list? And do you want to talk about it?*

*Rao:* I wanted to start an R&D initiative to work on the toughest engineering problems in the world that could make people's lives better. The idea was to hire 100 really intelligent scientists, researchers and engineers from the best institutes around the world and work on resolving difficult engineering problems. I had even considered handing over Pennar to the next rung of leaders much earlier, so I could have focused completely on this.

*A lot of your former employees, friends and colleagues have said that you said 'yes' too often to those who walked into your office with a request. Your thoughts.*

*Rao:* I have no regrets and would not have changed that.

*Your perspective on India and where it stands today.*

*Rao:* It is a great state with lots of potential, some of which has been realized, and more that will be realized in the future. The number of smart young people who are well-equipped with the technological tools today is encouraging and that, combined with an increasingly sophisticated ecosystem of capital, bodes well.

# Note from Nrupender Rao

I believed in entrepreneurship as a way to resolve national and global problems and viewed it as the mechanism to revolutionize job creation, standard-of-living rise, productivity growth and technological evolution. It is at the core of me to constantly encourage young people to think big.

My grounding in the teachings of Shri Ramakrishna and Swami Vivekananda led me to be a proponent of six values:

1. You are not limited and can accomplish anything that you want to set your mind to. You are the creator of your own destiny.
2. Hold all human beings in high esteem just as you would want to be held in high esteem, because all human beings—irrespective of religion, caste, creed or social and financial position—are worthy of respect.

3. Be strong and fearless. Believe that strength is life and weakness is death. Achieving excellence in all we do is the standard we must all strive towards.
4. To achieve your goals, you must follow the path that is right and truthful, even if it is difficult. Following the wrong path will not allow us to achieve the right results. Your motto must be 'Satyameva Jayate'.
5. Success belongs to the team. Work with your colleagues in a spirit of equality and cooperation. Leave no place for jealousy or envy.
6. Work hard with shraddha in your work. Your sadhana will be to be the best in whatever you do. In Swami Vivekananda's words, 'arise, awake and stop not till the goal is achieved'.

I want my life and experience to illustrate one truth: perseverance and determination are critical to achieving our dreams. When we set our sights on achieving great things, it is inevitable that we will slip and fall. I believe that in the face of boundless adversity and an ocean of rejection, you have to find it within yourself to stand up and keep fighting for your dreams. Anyone who decides to not give up and persist is ultimately destined to win.

# References


99 Corporates, Pennar Industries Limited, 17 May 2022, https://www.99corporates.com/Company-Overview/PENNAR-INDUSTRIES-LIMITED/CIN/L27109TG1975PLC001919

Adapt, Pennar Industries Limited, 17 May 2022, https://www.adapt.io/company/pennar-industries-limited

Barron's, Pennar Industries Limited, 17 May 2022, https://www.barrons.com/market-data/stocks/513228/company-people?countrycode=in&mod=quotes

Bloomberg, Joginapally Venkata Nrupender Rao, 17 May 2022, https://www.bloomberg.com/profile/person/15729488

BQ Prime, Pennar Industries Limited, 17 May 2022, https://www.bloombergquint.com/stock/242907/pennar-industries-ltd

Business Standard, 'Budget 2022: Indian Railways capex at all-time high of Rs 2.45 trillion', 2 February 2022, https://www.business-standard.com/budget/article/budget-

2022-indian-railways-capex-at-all-time-high-of-rs-2-45-trillion-122020101272_1.html

Business Standard, 'India's 2022 steel consumption seen strong amid muted prices, infra push', 4 January 2022, https://www.business-standard.com/article/companies/india-s-2022-steel-consumption-seen-strong-amid-muted-prices-infra-push-122010401102_1.html

Business Standard, 'India's crude steel output grows 18% to 118 MT in 2021, says Worldsteel', 30 January 2022, https://www.business-standard.com/article/economy-policy/india-s-crude-steel-output-grows-18-to-118-mt-in-2021-says-worldsteel-122013000645_1.html

Business Standard, 'JSW push to see Bhushan Power & Steel post best-ever performance in FY22', 27 January 2022,https://www.business-standard.com/article/companies/jsw-push-to-see-bhushan-power-steel-post-best-ever-performance-in-fy22-122012600646_1.html

Business Standard, 'Pennar Industries bags Rs 50-cr orders', 20 January 2013, https://www.business-standard.com/article/companies/pennar-industries-bags-rs-50-cr-orders-112112000138_1.html

Business Standard, 'Pennar Industries setting up unit in Chennai', 14 February 2013, https://www.business-standard.com/article/companies/pennar-industries-setting-up-unit-in-chennai-106111501019_1.html

Business Standard, 'Steel firms expect higher offtake from auto in Q4 after weak show earlier', 13 January 2022, https://www.business-standard.com/article/companies/steel-firms-expect-higher-offtake-from-auto-in-q4-after-weak-show-earlier-122011300690_1.html

BusinessLine, 'HMA Lifetime award for Nrupender Rao', 3 January 2019, https://www.thehindubusinessline.com/news/hma-lifetime-award-for-nrupender-rao/article25902692.ece

Care Ratings, Pennar Industries Limited, 5 April 2015, https://www.careratings.com/upload/CompanyFiles/PR/05042021071309_Pennar_Industries_Limited.pdf

Casemine, 'Consent order against Mr. J, Nrupender Rao', 5 November 2008, https://www.casemine.com/judgement/in/5d9b2e9b4a932678762df02b

Chartink, Pennar Industries Limited, 17 May 2022, https://chartink.com/stocks/penind.html

CII, Investment opportunities in Telangana, 17 May 2022,

https://www.cii.in/PhotoGalleryDetail.aspx?enc=FB

1+6I3SFq54ckGoFOQJJbIK29nWA0qhtJ9ISPAGnP+p1

m+NQCTM5JJti92oDKu7W4s6qX7Gfl7pIeW8ML2ifzLvsV5sdPypZq5n3RnspKOf8Gp4hBRE5GPaxX1gCxK8SbecNarwfACtP+Bnu1bcg+nxG/pIdHCLtsRX5TgpGos=

Cision PR Newswire, 'Pennar Industries Announced Buyback of Equity Shares', 15 November 2019, https://www.prnewswire.com/in/news-releases/pennar-industries-announced-buyback-of-equity-shares-801135122.html

Construction Week, 'Pennar Industries bags orders worth Rs 582 cr' 18 December 2021, https://www.constructionweekonline.in/projects-tenders/pennar-industries-bags-orders-worth-rs-582-cr

Craft, Pennar Industries Key Executives, 17 May 2022, https://craft.co/pennar-industries/executives

Crunchbase, Nrupender Rao, 17 May 2022, https://www.crunchbase.com/person/nrupender-rao-1718

Dalal Street Investment Journal, 'Pennar Industries zooms over 10 per cent on bagging new orders', 13 July 2021, https://www.dsij.in/dsijarticledetail/pennar-industries-zooms-over-10-per-cent-on-bagging-new-orders-19324

David Memorial Education Society, Leadership, 17 May 2022, http://www.davidmemorial.in/the-leadership/

DNA, 'Pennar Ind lines up share buyback', 17 May 2022, https://www.dnaindia.com/business/report-pennar-ind-lines-up-share-buyback-1251036

Dun & Bradstreet, Pennar Industries Ltd., 17 May 2022, https://www.dnb.com/business-directory/company-profiles.pennar_industries_limited.03e2cc2463176d2173ff3b4a36968cb3.html

Easyleadz, Pennar Industries Limited, 17 May 2022, https://www.easyleadz.com/company/pennar-industries

Economic Times, Pennar Industries Management Information, 17 May 2022, https://economictimes.indiatimes.com/pennar-industries-ltd/infocompanymanagement/companyid-13284.cms

EquityBulls, 'Pennar Industries' promoter releases 25 lakh pledged shares', 31 March 2020, https://equitybulls.com/category.php?id=264855

Financial Express, 'Economic Survey 2022: Next 10 years to see very high level of capex in railway sector', 31 January 2022, https://www.financialexpress.com/budget/economic-survey-2022-next-10-years-to-see-very-high-level-of-capex-in-railway-sector/2421195/

Financial Express, 'Economic Survey 2022: Railways to see jump in allocation', 31 January 2022, https://www.financialexpress.com/budget/economic-survey-2022-railways-to-see-jump-in-allocation/2421274/

Goodreturns, Directors Report of Pennar Industries Ltd., 31 March 2018, https://www.goodreturns.in/company/pennar-industries/director-report.html

Groww, Pennar Industries Limited, 17 May 2022, https://groww.in/stocks/pennar-industries-ltd

ICICI Direct, Pennar Industries Limited, 17 May 2022, https://www.icicidirect.com/stocks/pennar-industries-ltd-share-price

India Infoline, 'Mr. Nrupender Rao, Chairman, Pennar Industries Ltd', 30 August 2011, https://www.indiainfoline.com/article/research-leader-speak/mr-nrupender-rao-chairman-pennar-industries-ltd-113111403322_1.html

India Infoline, 'Pennar Industries hits record high after Group companies bag orders worth Rs 571 Cr', 13 July 2021, https://www.indiainfoline.com/article/news-top-story/pennar-industries-hits-record-high-after-group-companies-bag-orders-worth-rs571cr-121071300473_1.html

Indiamart, Pennar Industries Limited, 17 May 2022, https://www.indiamart.com/pennar-industries-limited-telangana/board-of-directors.html

Instafinancials, Joginapally Venkata Nrupender Rao, 17 May 2022, https://www.instafinancials.com/director/joginapally-venkata-nrupender-rao/00089922

Invest India, 'Budget 2022: What's in it for the Railways Sector?', 1 February 2022, https://www.investindia.gov.in/team-india-blogs/budget-2022-whats-it-railways-sector

Investing.com, Pennar Industries Limited, 17 May 2022, https://in.investing.com/equities/pennar-industries-ltd-company-profile

JustDial, Pennar Industries Limited, 17 May 2022, https://www.justdial.com/jdmart/Vijayawada/Pennar-Industries-Ltd-Near-Jrd-Tata-Industries-Auto-Nagar/0866PX866-X866-190706172158-R5A4_BZDET/catalogue

Justia, US Law, https://law.justia.com/cases/federal/appellate-courts/F2/466/945/424870/

Jyoti, Pennar Industries Limited, 17 May 2022, https://jyoti.co.in/clients/pennar-industries-limited/

Kompass, Pennar Industries Limited, 17 May 2022, https://in.kompass.com/c/pennar-industries-limited/in770569/

Livemint, 'Greenko Solar to acquire stake in Pennar's renewable energy unit', 15 August 2017, https://www.livemint.com/Companies/OSmvOxPZvmcvILwrNvLT9L/Greenko-Solar-to-acquire-stake-in-Pennars-renewable-energy.html

Livemint, 'Resurrecting Brand Hyderabad', 2 June 2015, https://www.livemint.com/Politics/hLaMOzbcWwlS8fEzxFvFNI/Resurrecting-Brand-Hyderabad.html

LKP Securities Limited, Pennar Industries Limited, 17 May 2022, https://www.lkpsec.com/company/pennar-industries-ltd/113228

Maharashtra Directory, Pennar Industries Limited, 17 May 2022, https://www.maharashtradirectory.com/companyinfo/pennar-industries-ltd-thane-64492.html

Market Watch, Pennar Industries Limited, 17 May 2022, https://www.marketwatch.com/investing/stock/513228/company-profile?countrycode=in

Moneycontrol, 'Pennar Inds standalone September 2021 net sales at Rs 493.16 crore, up 25.47% Y-o-Y', 12 November 2021, https://www.moneycontrol.com/news/business/earnings/pennar-inds-standalone-september-2021-net-sales-at-rs-493-16-crore-up-25-47-y-o-y-7712531.html

Moneycontrol, Pennar Industries Ltd., 17 May 2022, https://www.moneycontrol.com/company-facts/pennarindustries/management/pi28

MoneyWorks4Me, Pennar Industries Limited, 17 May 2022, https://www.moneyworks4me.com/indianstocks/small-cap/metals-mining/steel-iron-products/pennar-industries/company-info

MorningStar, Pennar Industries Limited, 17 May 2022, https://morningstar.in/stocks/0p0000rumt/nse-pennar-industries-ltd-shs-dematerialised/performance.aspx

MyCorporateInfo, Joginapally Venkata Nrupender Rao, 17 May 2022, http://www.mycorporateinfo.com/director/joginapally-venkata-nrupender-rao-89922

NCR, https://www.ncr.com/about/history

NDTV, Pennar Industries Ltd., 17 May 2022, https://www.ndtv.com/business/stock/pennar-industries-ltd_penind/reports-chairman-speech

NirmalBang, Pennar Industries Limited, 17 May 2022, https://www.nirmalbang.com/company/pennar-industries/113228

NSE India, Pennar Industries Limited Q4 & FY19 Result, 1 May 2019, https://www1.nseindia.com/corporate/PENIND_28052019111018_PennarIndustries_025.pdf

Outlook, 'Pennar's new avatar', https://www.outlookbusiness.com/perspective/pennars-new-avatar-949

Panjiva, 'Supply Chain Intelligence about: Pennar Industries Ltd.', 17 May 2022, https://panjiva.com/Pennar-Industries-Ltd/42495999

Pebs Pennar, Pennar Engineered Building Systems Limited, 2 September 2015, https://www.sebi.gov.in/sebi_data/attachdocs/1441687199427.pdf

Pennar Engineering Excellence, 'Pennar Industries Limited Q1 FY13 Results Conference Call', 25 July 2012, http://www.aceanalyser.com/Conference%20Call/113228_20120725.pdf

Pennar Enviro Limited, Management Team, 17 May 2022, http://pennarchemical.com/management.htm

Pennar Enviro, Management Team, 17 May 2022, https://pennarenviro.com/management_team.html

Pennar Global, Pennar Global Inc., 17 May 2022, https://pennarglobal.com/

Pocket News Alert, 'Mr. Nrupender Rao elected as Chairman of the CII Telangana for the year 2016-17', 16 March 2016, https://www.pocketnewsalert.com/2016/03/MR-

NRUPENDER-RAO-ELECTED-AS-CHAIRMAN-OF-THE-CII-TELANGANA-FOR-THE-YEAR-2016-17.html

PressReader, 'First in school, best in class', 21 April 2013, https://www.pressreader.com/india/deccan-chronicle/20130421/282553015726197

Projects Today, Pennar Industries Limited, 17 May 2022, https://www.projectstoday.com/Directory/Company/Pennar-Industries-Ltd

Rediff Moneywiz, Pennar Industries Limited, 17 May 2022, https://money.rediff.com/companies/Pennar-Industries-Ltd/15540012

Resource Inputs Pvt. Ltd., Leadership, 17 May 2022, https://resourceinputs.com/leadership/

Reuters, 'Pennar Industries gets shareholders' nod to re-appoint Nrupender Rao as chairman', 29 September 2017, https://www.reuters.com/article/brief-pennar-industries-gets-shareholder-idINFWN1MA0DX

Samco, Pennar Industries Limited, 17 May 2022, https://www.samco.in/share-price/pennar-industries-ltd/PENIND/INE932A01024

Simply Wall St., 'Investors in Pennar Industries have made a respectable return of 52% over the past year', 12 January 2022, https://simplywall.st/stocks/in/materials/nse-penind/pennarindustries-shares/news/investors-in-pennar-industries-nsepenind-have-made-a-respect

Skyscrapercity, 'Hyderabad Large & Small scale Manufacturing Industries updates', 30 July 2010, https://www.skyscrapercity.

com/threads/hyderabad-small-large-scale-industries-updates.1183377/

Smart-Investing, Pennar Industries Limited, 17 May 2022, https://www.smart-investing.in/main.php?Company=PENNAR+INDUSTRIES+LTD

The Hans India, 'Pennar Industries Q2 PAT sees multi-fold growth', 12 November 2021, https://www.thehansindia.com/business/pennar-industries-q2-pat-sees-multi-fold-growth-714911

The Hindu, 'Pennar Industries bags orders worth ₹517 cr.', 20 November 2020, https://www.thehindu.com/news/cities/Hyderabad/pennar-industries-bags-orders-worth-517-cr/article33144118.ece

The Indian Express, 'TDP-Congress Prajakutami: An alliance of a different kind', 6 November 2018, https://indianexpress.com/article/explained/telangana-assembly-elections-congress-tdp-alliance-prajakutami-k-chandrashekar-rao-5435401/

The Week, 'Pennar Industries to Scale up 'Build360' Retail Outlets for Branded Building Products', 2 April 2020, https://www.theweek.in/wire-updates/business/2019/03/26/pwr13--pennar%20industries%20limited.html

TheMachinist, 'Pennar Industries reports 25.8% y-o-y increase in Q1', 14 August 2019, https://www.themachinist.in/search?utf8=%E2%9C%93&query=pennar

Ticker Tape, Pennar Industries Limited, 17 May 2022, https://www.tickertape.in/stocks/pennar-industries-PENN?checklist=basic

Time, 'HYDERABAD: Silver Jubilee Durbar', 22 February 1937, https://content.time.com/time/subscriber/article/0,33009,770599,00.html

Tofler, Pennar Industries Limited, 16 May 2022, https://www.tofler.in/pennar-industries-limited/company/L27109TG1975PLC001919

TradeIndia, Pennar Industries Limited, 17 May 2022, https://www.tradeindia.com/Seller-8229088-Pennar-industries-limited/

Trendlyne, Pennar Industries Limited, 17 May 2022, https://trendlyne.com/equity/1020/PENIND/pennar-industries-ltd/

UNI, Nrupender elected Chairman of CII Telangana, 16 March 2016, http://www.uniindia.net/nrupender-elected-chairman-of-cii-telangana/business-economy/news/416949.html

Value Research, Pennar Industries Ltd., 17 May 2022, https://www.valueresearchonline.com/stocks/2900/pennar-industries-ltd/#snapshot

ValuePickr, Pennar Industries Limited, 17 May 2022, https://forum.valuepickr.com/t/pennar-industries-limited/12408

VCCircle, 'Pabrai Investment Funds pares stakes; Elevation sells Pennar Industries shares', 27 May 2021, https://www.vccircle.com/pabrai-investment-funds-pares-stakes-elevation-sells-pennar-industries-shares

Wikimapia, Pennar Industries Limited, 17 May 2022, http://wikimapia.org/1449686/Pennar-Industries-Pvt-Limited

World Scientific, Downsizing at Pennar Industries Limited, 1 August 2004, https://www.worldscientific.com/doi/10.1142/S0218927504000477

WSJ, Pennar Industries Ltd, 17 May 2022, https://www.wsj.com/market-data/quotes/IN/513228/company-people

Yahoo Finance, Pennar Industries Limited, 17 May 2022, https://finance.yahoo.com/quote/PENIND.NS/profile?p=PENIND.NS&guccounter=1&guce_referrer=aHR0cHM6Ly93d3cuZ29vZ2xlLmNvbS8&guce_referrer_sig=AQAAAM90waDu4nP15uJ1aPiSvQ-xS9hjBOMiX0_OH5eGdyRCLuU02RRP-nQgkd-XSp-cxIeOW-LgpcuIhI49LyRHnd5uZ_wgr1ZZw-udkNZcvKg27SQwb5pwpDKqrFzEArw6ivExtbxs0JBOGKYUC6-BWZTZSAnyhNfilAEG9lwNWDnD

ZaubaCorp, Pennar Industries Limited, 6 April 2022, https://www.zaubacorp.com/company/PENNAR-INDUSTRIES-LIMITED/L27109TG1975PLC001919

Zeebiz, Pennar Industries Limited, 17 May 2022, https://www.zeebiz.com/market/stocks/pennar-industries-ltd-pennarsteels

Zoominfo, Pennar Industries Limited, 17 May 2022, https://www.zoominfo.com/c/pennar-industries-limited/79463418

# Acknowledgements

The Rao family would like to acknowledge and thank a number of people who have prominently figured and provided support to Mr Nrupender Rao during the course of his life and across a variety of dimensions that include business, his early years, his personal journey and other facets.

Throughout his life, Mr Nrupender Rao has influenced and been influenced by a great number of people. In spite of their best efforts, the Rao family has conceded that many people, who have been important and critical contributors to Mr Nrupender Rao's journey and the Pennar Group's evolution as a company, have not been mentioned due to the large number of people that Mr Nrupender Rao worked and interacted with. The Rao family requests everyone's understanding in this regard.

Mr Nrupender Rao's extended family has always been a source of great support and strength to him in his personal life and his career. The Rao family would like to begin by extending their thanks to all members of his extended family. Some members who they would like to specifically mention are late J.V. Narsing Rao and late Radha Devi, late Rajah Chinna Rao and late Saraswati Inuganti, M.V. Rajeshwar Rao and Dr Ratnamala Rao, Dr Muralidhar and Dr Rekha Rao, Dr Ramdev and Renuka Rao, Dr Sampath and Dr Rupa Chennamaneni, Naresh Kumar and Saritha Rao, late Ramprakash Inuganti, Nalini Devi, Dr Surender and Srisudha Rao, K. Lavanya Kumar, Sridhar Chelikani, Subbarao Govardhanagiri and Dr Sudeepta Rao.

The Rao family would like to note that Mr Nrupender Rao had built strong lifelong relationships with several of his friends from school and university. Some of his closest friends who he remained in close contact with throughout his life were A.B. Bhushan, Dr Prithvipathi Rao, Prabhakar, Suresh Kulkarni, Ashok Shrivastava, J.K. Bihani, late Saumyendranath Maharaj Deogarh, Rajendra Bagrodia, Rajiv Tandon, Boka Sudarshan Reddy and Vala Dharamsagar.

Finally, throughout his professional and entrepreneurial career Mr Nrupender Rao was assisted by many of his colleagues, supporters and well wishers. He spoke often of how he believed his accomplishments were made possible only through their support. The Rao family would like to thank B. Kamalakar Rao, C. Koteshwar Rao, Dennis Mallace, Dr B. Karunakar, Ganesh Balakrishnan, K. Gopal, Koshy Verghese, late K.V.K. Raju, late C.D. Ramchandran, late N.J.

Yassasvy, M.B. Raju, Manish Sabharwal, Dr Chandrasekhar Sripada, P.K. Madhav, P.V. Rao, R. Rajamani, R.S. Sampath, Rajiv Dhar, Ravi and Vikram Chachra, Ravi Rambabu, R.V.S. Ramakrishna, Samad Nurus, Sunil Kuram, S.V. Ramchandar Rao, T.N.J. Raman, Venkatarama Raju, Vijay Mishra, Vijay N. Rao and Vijay Puljal.

Mr Nrupender Rao was also profoundly influenced by several individuals and thought leaders who went beyond the ambit of regular associations. The family would like to mention the close relationship he had with late Swami Ranganathananda, late Swami Vireshwaranandji, late Swami Jitatmanandji, late Kowtha Manohar, late James David and late Dr N.C.B. Nath.

Lastly, the family would also like to note Pavan C. Lall's contributions to the biography. The goal of the biography is to tell Mr Nrupender Rao's story objectively and without bias. Pavan's graciousness, candour and hard work shine through in his work. The family is grateful to Pavan for the rigour with which he approached the task including the many hours of interviews conducted, his exhaustive study of Mr Nrupender Rao's notes and his visits to so many places of importance to Mr Rao, including Pennar's factories, offices and the Ramakrishna Math. In order to author this book, Pavan committed himself to understanding Mr N. Rao and the Pennar story and the result is this book which, in our view, is an accurate and faithful account of Mr N. Rao's life and the principles he lived by.

The Rao family is grateful to all of Mr Nrupender Rao's extended family members, his friends and his colleagues, partners and associates for the role they played in his life and for their contributions. They believe that it is on the foundation of these relationships that Mr Nrupender Rao built his life and his work.

# About the Author

**Pavan C. Lall** is a Mumbai-based author and journalist who has written for *Fortune* magazine's Indian edition, the *Dallas Business Journal*, *Moneycontrol*, *Mint* and the *Business Standard*, on the automotive sector, private equity, real estate, storied conglomerates and more. A winner of the Citi Journalistic Excellence Award in 2016, what really drives him, besides very fast German cars, is telling great stories that have not been heard.

Born in Kolkata, and schooled in Darjeeling, he got his college education in Texas where he worked for a decade. He was also featured on the Netflix show *Bad Boy Billionaires*. His second book, *Yes Man: The Untold Story of Rana Kapoor* (December 2020), was shortlisted for the Gaja Capital Business Book award in 2021.

In recent years, he has also served as an advisor to Nykaa, the e-commerce unicorn that had the most successful IPO in India in 2021, and also provided analysis and commentary for the Financial Times as a specialist on Indian tycoons.